WOMEN'S WEALTH AND WOMEN'S WRITING IN EARLY MODERN ENGLAND

Women and Gender in the Early Modern World

Series Editors: Allyson Poska and Abby Zanger

In the past decade, the study of women and gender has offered some of the most vital and innovative challenges to scholarship on the early modern period. Ashgate's new series of interdisciplinary and comparative studies, 'Women and Gender in the Early Modern World', takes up this challenge, reaching beyond geographical limitations to explore the experiences of early modern women and the nature of gender in Europe, the Americas, Asia, and Africa. Submissions of single-author studies and edited collections will be considered.

Titles in this series include:

English Printing, Verse Translation, and the Battle of the Sexes,
1476–1557
Anne E.B. Coldiron

Love, Lust, and License in Early Modern England
Illicit Sex and the Nobility
Johanna Rickman

Women, Identities and Communities in Early Modern Europe
Oral Traditions and Gender
Edited by Stephanie Tarbin and Susan Broomhall

Masculinity and Emotion in Early Modern English Literature
Jennifer Vaught

Figuring Modesty in Feminist Discourse Across the Americas,
1633–1700
Tamara Harvey

Women's Wealth and Women's Writing in Early Modern England
'Little Legacies' and the Materials of Motherhood

ELIZABETH MAZZOLA
City College of the City University of New York, USA

LONDON AND NEW YORK

First published 2009 by Ashgate Publishing

Published 2016 by Routledge
2 Park Square, Milton Park, Abingdon, Oxon OX14 4RN
711 Third Avenue, New York, NY 10017, USA

Routledge is an imprint of the Taylor & Francis Group, an informa business

Copyright © 2009 Elizabeth Mazzola

Elizabeth Mazzola has asserted her moral right under the Copyright, Designs and Patents Act, 1988, to be identified as the author of this work.

All rights reserved. No part of this book may be reprinted or reproduced or utilised in any form or by any electronic, mechanical, or other means, now known or hereafter invented, including photocopying and recording, or in any information storage or retrieval system, without permission in writing from the publishers.

Notice:
Product or corporate names may be trademarks or registered trademarks, and are used only for identification and explanation without intent to infringe.

British Library Cataloguing in Publication Data
Mazzola, Elizabeth
Women's wealth and women's writing in early modern England: 'little legacies' and the materials of motherhood. –
(Women and gender in the early modern world)
    1. Elizabeth, I, Queen of England, 1533–1603 2. Mary, Queen of Scots, 1542–1587 3. Shrewsbury, Elizabeth Hardwick Talbot, Countess of, 1527?–1608 4. Stuart, Arabella, Lady, 1575–1615 5. English literature – Early modern, 1500–1700 – History and criticism 6. English literature – Early modern, 1500–1700 – Women authors 7. Women intellectuals – England – History – 16th century 8. Social networks – England – History – 16th century 9. Personal property – England – History – 16th century
    I. Title
    820.9'9287'09031

Library of Congress Cataloging-in-Publication Data
Mazzola, Elizabeth.
  Women's wealth and women's writing in early modern England : 'little legacies' and the materials of motherhood / by Elizabeth Mazzola.
    p. cm. — (Women and gender in the early modern world)
  Includes bibliographical references and index.
  ISBN 978-0-7546-6663-9 (alk. paper)
  1. English literature—Early modern, 1500–1700—History and criticism. 2. Women—England—Economic conditions. 3. English literature—Women authors—History and criticism. 4. Property—England—History. 5. Women and literature—England—History—16th century. 6. Women and literature—England—History—17th century. 7. Women—England—Economic conditions. 8. Economics in literature. I. Title.

  PR428.W63M39 2009
  820.9'9287—dc22

                                                 2008028591

ISBN 9780754666639 (hbk)

For Alison, Pamela, and Jim, so good at keeping me company

Contents

List of Illustrations		*viii*
Acknowledgments		*x*
Introduction		1
1	*Miroir or Glasse*	13
2	Borrowed Robes	33
3	"Manifest housekeepers"	49
4	Strange Bedfellows	71
5	"Girles aflote"	87
Bibliography		*109*
Index		*123*

List of Illustrations

Frontispiece   'LADY ARABELLA STUART AGED 23 MONTHS' by Anon 1577. The little girl, formally dressed, is holding a doll. Hardwick Hall, The National Trust. Copyright NTPL / John Hammond

1.1   Jane Bostocke's 1598 sampler. V & A Images / Victoria and Albert Museum   15

1.2   Autograph letter from Alathea Talbot Howard, ca. 1606–1608. The Pierpont Morgan Library, New York   17

1.3   Embroidered cover for Elizabeth's *Glasse*. MS Cherry 36. The Bodleian Library / University of Oxford   23

1.4   Elizabeth's dedication of *The Glasse* to Katherine Parr. MS Cherry 36, fol. 2r. The Bodleian Library / University of Oxford   25

2.1   Queen Elizabeth I by an unknown artist (1600). The National Portrait Gallery, London   37

3.1   Mary Stuart's embroidered image of a hand with pruning knife. V & A Images / Victoria and Albert Museum   58

3.2   Marigold turning to the sun with Mary Stuart's cipher. V & A Images / Victoria and Albert Museum   60

3.3   Mary Stuart's Sea Moonke. V & A Images / Victoria and Albert Museum   62

3.4   Mary Stuart's Reindeer and Milkmaid. V & A Images / Victoria and Albert Museum   64

5.1   New Hall at Hardwick. Copyright NTPL / Geoff Morgan   88

5.2   One of Bess's initials adorning New Hall at Hardwick. Copyright NTPL / David Levenson   91

5.3	One of Bess's needleworked panels with the monogram of her second husband. V & A Images / Victoria and Albert Museum	101
5.4	The Cavendish hanging, including several of Bess's panels and Mary Stuart's royal monogram. V & A Images / Victoria and Albert Museum	102

Acknowledgments

This project has drawn on the work of many other scholars, and I am particularly grateful for the advice and ideas shared by Sara Jayne Steen, Laurie Ellinghausen, Thomas Kuehn, Mihoko Susuki, Susan Frye, Retha Warnicke, Erin Murphy, Jane Lawson, Peter Herman, and especially Germaine Warkentin, who first got me thinking about the clothing of royal sisters and directed me to the stunning work on Elizabeth Tudor's wardrobe by Janet Arnold; even longer ago, Jane Donawerth encouraged me to think about early modern women writers, and I want to acknowledge her support all these years later, with tremendous thanks. The prodigious work of Margaret J. M. Ezell on early modern women's manuscript culture has also been invaluable to this study. Two research grants provided by The City University Professional Staff Congress allowed me the time to read and to write, and The Rifkind Center of the City College of New York funded a course release, generously permitting me the opportunity to assemble the argument. The Rifkind Center also provided funds to cover the costs of reproducing many of the images used in this book. My editor Erika Gaffney has encouraged this project from the outset, and I wish to thank her as well as anonymous reader for Ashgate Press for their invaluable help. Jacqui Cornish, Meredith Coeyman, and Whitney Feininger at Ashgate provided additional assistance, and I thank them for their kindness.

I also am indebted to the scholars, curators, and archivists who always responded to my queries and requests with an abundance of information and assistance: Leslie Fields, at the Morgan Library, supplied me with a copy of Alathea Talbot Howard's beautiful letter almost immediately upon receipt of a humble letter from me; Erika Ingham at the National Portrait Gallery provided rich materials on Mary Stuart's wardrobe and Tudor iconography; Alison J. Carter of the Hampshire County Museum, and Aileen Ribiero and Margaret Scott of the Courtauld Institute responded to questions about Elizabeth's coronation robes with great skill and much patience; Arbella Stuart of the NTPL granted me permission to use the picture of her namesake which adorns this book's cover; and Betsy Walsh provided valuable assistance with the Cavendish-Talbot manuscripts at the Folger Shakespeare Library. Perhaps I am most beholden to Evelyn Bodden and the interlibrary loan staff at the CCNY Cohen Library for their regular and patient indulgence.

Portions of this book were presented at The Huntington Library and at the New York University English Department Colloquium as well as at meetings of the Society for the Study of Women in the Renaissance, The Shakespeare Colloquium at Fairleigh Dickinson University, The University of Maryland's conference on "Attending to Early Modern Women," and The Modern Language Association.

Acknowledgments xi

I am grateful for the invitations extended by Ernesto Gilman, Harry Keyishian, Corinne S. Abate, and George Gorse to share my work at these venues, and for the suggestions made by Elizabeth Bearden, Erna Kelly, John Archer, Hal Momma, Susan O'Malley, and Elizabeth Hageman in attendance at those hearings. The first graders at St. Francis Cathedral School in Metuchen, NJ, were an especially eager audience, and I want to thank Mrs. Marilou Rizzo and Miss Michelle Racavich for the opportunity to share my work with their classes. I am also indebted to the anonymous readers at *Early Modern Women: An Interdisciplinary Journal* and at *Exemplaria*, who read over versions of chapter two and three, respectively. Their comments were extraordinarily careful, learned, and generous, and I have prized their help: I hope these readers find their ideas put to good use, although, of course, all the failings and tangles that remain here are my own. I also thank the editors of *Early Modern Women* and *Exemplaria* for their permission to reprint materials, as well as Oxford University Press, which allowed me to quote from Sara Jayne Steen's 1995 edition of Arbella Stuart's letters, and the Medieval and Renaissance Text Society, which permitted me to quote from Peter C. Herman's translation of Mary Stuart's poems.

I have been fortunate to work with the students and faculty at The City College of New York, and I particularly want to thank Patricia Brody, Mikhal Dekel, Paul Oppenheimer, and Mark Mirsky for their continued friendship and advice. Fred Reynolds, Dean of Humanities & Arts at City College, has been a source of support for many years, and it is impossible for me to imagine my life as a scholar or teacher without his help. I also want to thank Selma Erhardt for her unflagging interest in this project.

I have dedicated this book to my daughters and husband. That I can share so many stories with them has been a constant source of inspiration, and that they always want to know what happens *next* has been one of their many precious gifts to me.

December 2008
Metuchen, New Jersey

Introduction

> But it will be counted discretion in you, and confirme theyr good opinion of me if, you require them to bring all the testimonies they can. as somm picture or handwriting of the Lady Jane Gray whose hand I know. and she sent hir sister a booke at hir death which weare the very best they could bring.[1]

In one of Arbella Stuart's (1575–1615) many letters, written at a desperate time when she had been confined by Queen Elizabeth to the strict care of her grandmother, Bess of Hardwick, she outlines a daring plan for escape that includes detailed instructions for the use of women's writings. Stuart urges the Earl of Hertford to bring a handful of male retainers along with a cache of writings authored by the fifteen-year-old Lady Jane Grey, herself imprisoned (and later beheaded) for her presumption of sovereign power almost fifty years before. That something written by a long-dead and still-scandalized female relation (the sister of the Earl's first wife) would be preserved seems odd, even risky, but these documents recorded familial history, including the royal claims of one of its members: they were not merely heirlooms, as Arbella clearly recognizes, even if their status is equal to "somm picture or handwriting." Indeed, Arbella wants to have them *seen,* not *read,* a desire especially puzzling to literary critics. Merely having in one's possession something that Jane Grey had produced could be damning to Arbella, herself a native heir to Elizabeth's throne, who was now being punished by the Queen for similar reasons, years earlier incurring Elizabeth's displeasure after the seventeen-year-old Stuart was allegedly flirting with the nineteen-year-old Earl of Essex during a visit to court. That Arbella sees Lady Jane Grey's writing as a useful object, something which offers "testimony"—and that Arbella can recognize the hand and identify its provenance—reveals much, I think, about both the purposes and audience of women's writing in early modern England: who gets to handle or even read it, of course, but also how its meanings are transmitted and shared, and how its designs are construed primarily in terms of advancing some other woman's purposes or needs.

The value of early modern women's writing, in other words, was similar to that of other goods and services that women circulated or bequeathed at this time, like Lady Jane Grey's Greek New Testament, sent to her sister Catherine at her death.[2] To be sure, women's wealth could take a variety of shapes. Much of it was personal property collaboratively produced and exchanged, like those things that legally comprised a wife's paraphernalia and were, therefore, not subject to a husband's

---

[1]   Stuart's instructions were given in Letter 3 to John Dodderidge for Edward Seymour, Earl of Hertford. See the edition prepared by Steen (1994) 121.

[2]   Details are supplied in the notes accompanying Steen's (1994) edition (p. 121).

scrutiny or control, such as candlesticks, jewels, pots, tapestries, combs, stockings, ribbons, chairs, pillows, glassware, gloves or the services of a midwife, even a single plate, handed down for special use.[3] Those objects made up the bulk of what women owned or shared, and if their possessions might also occasionally include livestock or cash, women's wealth was primarily material in nature—sewn, copied, embroidered, "trauncelated," or otherwise crafted by hand. Rather than enriching the maker or owner, these goods sustained the world of female kin, transmitting not the authority of a single person but the power of this set of relationships.[4]

Jennifer Summit (2004) includes women's letters in this collection of goods, suggesting that when "read within the communal structures of the early modern household, women's letters do not offer autobiographies of individual selves so much as they do maps of relationships that extend outward into broader social and textual networks" (p. 202). Literacy in the early modern period could mean the ability to read or the ability to read Latin, legal documents or the secretary hand but, for women, literacy more often involved the process of making female ties legible: women who wrote were probably less interested in their status or activities as writers, more concerned with the transmission of valuable things and enforcement of kin ties.[5] The female networks Summit describes thus also tell us about the economics, aesthetics, and literature of the period—about which material

---

[3] The nature of this wealth, as well as the rules surrounding its accumulation and transmission, are explored by Erickson (1993). According to Cavallo, the fact that early modern women overwhelmingly left things rather than land or money "makes clear how limited women's property was. The range of objects they bequeathed—and thus the range of objects they believed were really 'theirs'—was extremely restricted; it was confined to a very narrowly circumscribed area of household space, a space which seems almost an extension of their bod[ies]" (pp.40–42). I would propose, however, that it is exactly from such a close association with female bodies and female spaces that this small-scale property has such wide-ranging influence, even magical powers; certainly Shakespeare alludes to such wealth in his picture of Othello's handkerchief or of Hermione's mantle, which identifies an abandoned daughter, sixteen years later.

[4] See Newman's (1996) description of this "polity." Virginia Woolf conjured up a foremother in Shakespeare's sister, only to imagine Judith Shakespeare as cruelly obliterated in the rush of commerce (p. 48). But more recent scholars have suggested that women were not by definition impoverished in the early modern period. As Kuehn reminds us, "not all wealth is or was alike" (p. 74). In addition, women of all classes probably had things to offer each other because wealth was tied more to labor or maker than to the object, as Parker and Pollock explain. Similar claims have been introduced by literary critics analyzing the way early modern women's culture took shape in a world daily reproduced by the preparation of food and cloth, and marked by the care and exchange of items typically not governed by or important to men; see, for instance, Wall (2002, pp.7–9); and Korda (2002). That much of this women's wealth should be seen as maternal wealth is explored by Frye (2000).

[5] For an exploration of midwives as comprising one such circle, see Hellwarth (p.44). That the authority women crafted and wielded as writers was similarly motivated by social and economic aims rather than literary ones is forcefully explored by Julie Crawford (2006 B).

Introduction 3

objects had special value; how these objects were made, exchanged, or shared; and what kinds of discourse supported their values and guaranteed their transmission.

That things might hold valuable information about people seems unlikely to us, but then, in an early modern world without banks or enough specie, material goods accommodated a variety of meanings, so that wealth transmitted wishes, obligations, ambitions. The material nature of this world is not a reflection of other concerns: it is the shape of them. Karen Newman (1996) points out the ubiquity of things in the world of sixteenth-century letters, for instance. She claims that to name "innumerable, miscellaneous objects" in these letters is to "establish familiar possession, to produce property" (p. 140). Nowadays we are accustomed to abstract subjects from objects and to isolate people from everything else in the world about them.[6] But, as historian Thomas J. Kuehn reminds us, there is nothing intrinsic about human relations. The ties that link people together are narrated by histories of meanings and demands and accompanied by inventories of gifts and services. The bonds of nature are thus always calculated by objects, made real and intelligible through stuff.[7]

This book explores the ways that women's writings in the early modern period concern their wealth, whether we define that wealth as goods and services, the influence and kin ties women accumulated through marriages and remarriages, real property (land) to which they typically had little access, or moveables (their paraphernalia) over which women might wield enormous power.[8] We should also include income from investments as well as earnings in this picture of resources available to women (including writers and prostitutes), an economy which underpins the "polity" Newman (1996) describes (p. 140). My claim is that women's writings not only describe but manage this wealth, as well as the women's networks this wealth fosters.

If we have been taught by recent critics to understand Lady Anne Clifford's (1590–1676) coming of age—her construction of herself as subject and as author as closely aligned throughout her life and within her family as a property battle (see Crawford [2006 A] and Klein [2001]), perhaps the same is true for all women at this time. I center here, though, on the long and troubled relationship among four English noblewomen, Queen Elizabeth herself (1533–1603), Elizabeth Talbot, the

---

[6]   Kinship in particular may be inherently tied up with property relations, as Crawford (2006 A) explains.

[7]   Kuehn's thinking has been crucial for my own, especially his suggestion that many of our assumptions about women's experience in the early modern period are "embedded in modern Western individualism" and thus centered on principles of "individual freedom and self-determination." But women's "personhood," Kuehn claims, "was relational and not individualistic," "not intrinsically unique" (pp. 59–60). See also Strathern (p. 298), quoted by Kuehn.

[8]   Harris (2002) discusses some of the legal loopholes exploited by aristocratic women and their families, thereby "muting," for instance, some of the inequities of primogeniture (pp.132–3). Harris's impressive research has been invaluable to my study.

Countess of Shrewsbury (more commonly known as Bess of Hardwick) (1527–1608), and Elizabeth's cousin Mary Stuart (1542–1587), herself imprisoned by the Queen for nearly sixteen years and placed under the care of Bess and her husband, George Talbot, the Earl of Shrewsbury. The fourth member of this group, Arbella Stuart, was a granddaughter of the Shrewsburys and niece of Mary Stuart as her father was Mary's brother-in-law Charles; Arbella was, therefore, a princess of the blood with a legitimate claim to Elizabeth's throne, at least in the eyes of many Catholic supporters during both Elizabeth's and her successor's reigns. The ties between Elizabeth, Bess, Mary, and Arbella are frequently strained, sometimes nearly broken, but they never unravel completely; instead, and for almost forty years, these links organize both domestic life and courtly culture, offering a reliable lens through which to view Elizabethan politics and the succession crisis, as well as the no less dramatic dynamics and conflicts that characterized many aristocratic households. The goods and favors they traded, probably presented—and typically understood by us—as simple and private exchanges of gifts, are powerful means of establishing and honoring dynastic claims and political debts as well.[9] What seems to signal affection among these women, in other words, may more deeply indicate resentment, misprision, or desire, and their ties can be manipulated to conduct the business of a petitioner, landlord, claimant, or captive.

That gifts among these four women represented claims as well as deferrals of affection also suggests something else—that there really was no larger world beyond the household, at least in the early modern period;[10] they illuminate as well the vagaries and vicissitudes of female authority, the carefully constructed nature of ties between women, and some of the crucial economic features of early modern mothering, for women of all classes. I would also propose that the particular connections among this strangely knit group of women—relations but also competitors, incredibly advantaged by the standards of their time but unusually positioned to feel Elizabeth's wrath and her warmth—provide us with a key to the larger world of women writers and readers slowly taking shape in the early modern period, to the ways that women might think about and learn from each other, and how such knowledge or influence could be shared in England's kitchens, bedchambers, and sewing circles.[11] If Princess Elizabeth Tudor's 1544 translation of a poem by Marguerite de Navarre supplies the author (and its readers) with one point of entry into this world, Aemilia Lanyer's 1611 "Description of Cooke-ham" is an elegy for its demise.

---

[9]   King offers details about a similar circle of women surrounding Parr. For a description of these practices in terms of anthropological models of gift-exchange, see Donawerth.

[10]   Harris (1982) takes up this issue explicitly (pp. 144–5).

[11]   Some details are offered by Snook, who forcefully argues, for instance, that to write or read in the early modern period meant assuming a position in a wider, older world of believers, thinkers, and philosophers all familiar with numerous texts including the Bible and treatises on animal husbandry and minor surgery, as well as grammatical and devotional exercises.

Introduction 5

***

The relationship between Elizabeth, Bess, Mary, and Arbella has yet to be fully explored, although Sarah Gristwood has recently characterized the association in terms of a "curious pattern, like an irregular diamond, its four corners bearing each a miniature of the four women whose destinies were intertwined, . . . two of the Tudor 'type' and two of the Stuart."[12] To be sure, my focus on this "curious pattern" concentrates on a handful of women at the uppermost reaches of Elizabethan society and politics, women who—with the exception of Bess—were unusually learned, formally trained, and on speaking terms with several ministers of state. They may seem utterly exceptional and, in some instances, unrepresentative of the women of their time. But in other ways the four women can be seen as successful models of what other early modern mothers and daughters were trying to achieve with each other. Interestingly, all four women were single women, at least for a large part of their lives, and relations with male kin—husbands, fathers or brothers—were thin, absent, or temporary.[13] Each of them, indeed, lived widowed, unmarried, or otherwise alone for a significant part of their lives. What remains constant is the pull and support of their female connections, along with the threats to and jealousy incurred by them. Many of their writings, including letters, wills, and speeches, even the iconography available in their needlework, announce and strain under these ties.

Other maternal figures cast their shadows here, Katherine Parr, Marguerite de Navarre, Mary of Guise, and Mary Tudor among them; but Elizabeth and Bess, Mary and Arbella respond to each other over and over again in the raw language of material things. To be sure, as one of the richest women in England, Bess was probably the most fluent in this language: the contents of one of her houses alone included, among other treasures, "a Counterpoynt of China cloth of gold," "Curtins of red cloth," "turkie Carpetes," a "quition of cloth of gold," a "vallans Indented with three little guilded knobs," "too brass Chafing dishes," a broken bell, and a stoole pan.[14] But all four women imagine their relationships in terms of legacies, with the rhetoric and anxieties that gifts between mothers and daughters impose, as well as the oft-repeated wish—as Princess Elizabeth proffers in a New Year's present to her stepmother—that the recipient would not only accept but mend her humble gift. What follows below is a rough outline of these four women's collective history and efforts, something to be explored in greater detail in the chapters which follow. I refer throughout to the poetry and other writings, clothing, and needlework that they exchanged with, borrowed from, or made for each other.

---

[12]   See Gristwood's preface.

[13]   My understanding and use of the term "singlewomen" is indebted to the studies anthologized by Bennett and Froide; in this volume Froide, however, suggests a more important difference than the one between married and singlewomen is between never-married and ever-married women (including, thus, the widowed) (pp. 236–7).

[14]   Levey (2001) has edited the inventories of Bess's vast holdings; see especially pages 33–4.

6 *Women's Wealth and Women's Writing in Early Modern England*

***

Mary Tudor was well acquainted with Bess and her second husband, Sir William Cavendish, a remarkably rich and successful officer at both her father's and brother's courts.[15] After Cavendish's death, Bess would marry Sir William St. Loe, who had long been a member of Princess Elizabeth's household and who was, almost immediately after Mary's death, appointed captain of Elizabeth's personal guard. Elizabeth's largesse to the couple would continue; immediately after the marriage, Bess was made a Lady of the Privy Chamber, "undoubtedly," Mary Lovell maintains, as "a wedding gift from the Queen" (p. 148).

By the time of Bess's fourth marriage to George Talbot (after St. Loe's sudden death), she had three sons in school, two married daughters and an unmarried daughter, along with considerable property, courtly connections, and the deep affection of her Queen (Lovell, p. 39). Just two years after the Talbot marriage, Elizabeth entrusted the couple with the care of Mary Stuart, the Scottish Queen who had fled her country after the mysterious death of her second husband. Bess was to spend the next sixteen years in close contact with Mary Stuart, needleworking and gossiping, more a confidante than a jailer, it sometimes appeared, at least in the first years of Mary's imprisonment. Indeed, as James Daybell explains, Mary's own information network in England was formidable enough to arouse the attentions of Sir Francis Walsingham, the founder of the English secret service.[16] During her long years under house arrest, Mary had retainers, priests, musicians, laundresses, and a handful of small animals always in attendance, along with a chair and cloth of state: her prison was lavish if damp and remote, and her housekeeping expenses extravagant. George Talbot was increasingly forced to cover costs out of his own huge pockets, and he and Bess frequently quarreled over expenditures. Rumors that Mary had seduced George also troubled husband and wife; and Talbot was allegedly angered as well by reports that Bess and Mary were conspiring against Elizabeth.

Actually, Bess's loyalties to Mary Stuart and to her Queen during these sixteen years are extremely unclear, especially after she and Stuart arrange for one of Bess's daughters to wed Charles Stuart in 1574, despite Elizabeth's express wishes against the union. As punishment, Margaret Lennox, Charles' mother (Mary's mother-in-law) was sent to the Tower, and Bess summoned to London.[17] The offspring of the forbidden union is Arbella, who was raised by Bess after Arbella's mother dies when the child is only four years old. Early on, Bess will petition

---

[15] For information on Bess's life and circle, I rely on Durant and the more recent biography by Lovell. Additional details about Bess's wealth and possessions are provided by Levey (1998).

[16] See Daybell (2004). Connections between Mary's loose confederation of spies and Sir Francis Walsingham's efforts to break their ring are detailed by Plowden.

[17] In contrast with what other biographers claim, Lovell says that "[d]espite being ordered to London, there is no surviving record that Bess spent any time in the Tower in January 1575, if, indeed, she went to London at all that winter" (pp. 249–50).

Introduction 7

Elizabeth for additional funds to finance Arbella's education, clothing, and grooming, expenses all incurred, Bess assumes, as part of the training of a royal heir. The Queen resists these demands, however, and invites Bess and Arbella to London on only a few occasions. When the teen-aged Arbella creates trouble at court in the winter of 1592, even this rare privilege is revoked. Placed under house arrest—much like her aunt Mary Stuart twenty years earlier—Arbella eventually concocts a scheme to hasten her release, proposing to the Seymour family that she marry Hertford's grandson Edward, another alliance expressly forbidden by the Queen. The plan predictably arouses Elizabeth's attention and Bess's ire, and the constraints upon Arbella are increased. When Arbella is interrogated by one of Elizabeth's councilors, she further complicates things by confessing a romance with the King of Scots. Old, weary, and deathly ill, Elizabeth seems to guess at Arbella's intentions and finally permits Arbella to move south, away from her strict grandmother's remote estate. Arbella's frustration (or ingratitude) continues, however, and she refuses to attend Elizabeth's funeral weeks later, even though, as the Queen's closest relative, she is Elizabeth's chief mourner. Bess had disinherited Arbella after her plans to marry Seymour were exposed, but apparently reconsiders on her deathbed and leaves Arbella a small inheritance when she dies in 1608. Arbella herself dies only a few years later at the age of forty, imprisoned in the Tower for her secret marriage to William Seymour, Edward's younger brother, an alliance contracted despite James' explicit disapproval.

***

The brief history offered above seems to offer a sorry set of entanglements, but I also read in them a strange and revealing account of how early modern women might imagine themselves, repeatedly, sometimes painfully, as mothers and daughters, rivals and authors, sovereigns and heirs, all actively negotiating the possession of a world of kin and things that they have shaped together. Little wonder that, as Adrienne Rich drily notes, the "idea of maternal power has been domesticated" in the modern period (p. 68). We need to suspend the "central metaphor" of patriarchalism, which, as Rich and Wendy Wall (2002) similarly suggest, obscures other models of social influence and familial organization if we want to identify the social and economic power that successful mothers wield, especially in societies that precede our own. The historian Barbara Harris (2002) has explored some of the economic requirements of early modern mothering in her study of the generation of mothers and wives before the reign of Elizabeth, but Harris separates pecuniary matters and political ambitions from the love and care mothers are also supposed to bestow:

> The structure and goals of aristocratic families created a class-specific, historically distinctive form of motherhood. With the exception of the last stages of their pregnancies and lyings-in, the priorities of aristocratic families meant that wives' relationships with their husbands, social and managerial functions, and duties at court took precedence over their obligations as mothers. Aristocratic mothers routinely delegated the physical care of their infants and young children

to servants and placed little weight on the importance of daily contact with them. They concentrated instead on ensuring that their adolescent and adult children possessed the property and connections they needed to maintain their position in their class and contribute to their families' advancement in the next generation. (p. 100)

That the two projects might be construed as antithetical to each other makes clear, I think, how different early modern mothers' powers and goals are from our own (constantly changing) ideas about mothering.[18] Some historians, as Harris notes, have argued that early modern mothers privileged the care of older children over that of younger ones because of high infant mortality rates. But perhaps a mother's influence and skills could best be utilized in organizing the rest of her children's lives, leaving the more physical demands of early childhood to other women like wet-nurses, with fewer resources at their disposal. There is little obvious record of Bess's affections for her children and step-children, for instance, but a remarkably exhaustive catalog of their bills for items that included stylish French hoods and waterproof wollens, "knitted waistcoats" for babies (rather than the more typical swaddling cloths) and sugar coated nuts (see Levey, 2000, pp. 15–18).

Just as strange as the way moral imperatives seem to be advanced and animated by material things is the way that early modern individuals—male and female alike—appear to identify with or locate themselves in extensive worlds of friends, kin, and neighbors. Our own world is much smaller, more inner-directed, more immediate in its rewards, with little sense of all the things people might share with each other. No wonder that our picture of the early modern woman writer is of someone unique or aberrant and an exception to the early modern rules of female illiteracy, subordination, and intellectual disability, whose writings suggest resistance, impoverishment and alienation rather than community, property, or influence. But we are increasingly discovering numbers of early modern women who wrote from a variety of classes, backgrounds, and purposes; further study often reveals how what they wrote was somehow designed to support and substantiate the world of women around them, to invite some return of feeling or labor. Letters, according to Jennifer Summit (2004) were "perhaps the defining genre of the household," but this household, she elaborates, was itself a "centre of writing,"[19] for the many other records that women left behind, chronicling New Year's gifts

---

[18]   That the circulation of women's wealth contributes to the "reproduction of mothering" that Chodorow describes is one of my central aims.

[19]   These important studies include Ezell (1993), who focuses on the "social literary culture" of early modern women (p. 124); Klein (1997); and Fleming. The collaborative nature of women's aesthetic productions and the consequences of this collaboration on academic study have been explored by Mainardi. See also the discussion of household letters in Summit (2004), where she claims "[l]etters do not merely represent material culture . . . but participate in it as objects themselves whose material modes of fashioning, use, and exchange hold meanings that exceed the limits of what they actually say" (p. 202).

Introduction 9

and outlining recipes, organizing mother's advice or inventorying households, similarly evoke a larger world of maternal influence and female authority, a world where the moral and material constitute each other, where women's ties are constantly reaffirmed and reproduced.

***

In the chapters which follow, I trace the peculiar nature of these ties, the material goods and services they transmit, and the kind of influence that women, often working together, were understood to have and to share, socially, morally, politically, economically, and on paper. Chapter 1, *"Miroir or Glasse,"* explores how the education of early modern daughters—ostensibly geared toward the training of wives and household managers—shapes and informs a more complex relation to their mothers. Indeed, the learning documented in many young women's letters, needlework samplers, primers, poems, and prayer translations often represents a maternal tie that is conflicted or ambivalent, rewritten by piety, or transformed through rivalry. I focus particularly on the carefully prepared translation of Marguerite de Navarre's devotional poetry undertaken by Elizabeth Tudor as a New Year's gift for her stepmother, the 1544 *Miroir or Glasse of the Synneful Soule*, given to Katherine Parr when the princess was eleven years old. I place Elizabeth's translation alongside the long-neglected but once famous *Hecatodistichon* (1550), a series of Latin distichs jointly written on the occasion of Marguerite's death by Reformist sisters Anne, Margaret, and Jane Seymour (roughly eighteen, sixteen, and nine years old, respectively), which strangely center upon a French Catholic progenitor. Both works reveal much about how the accomplishments of precocious and privileged daughters in the early modern period were motivated by a proper reckoning of kin ties, familial obligations, and maternal influences, dynastic politics carefully aligned with female genealogy. But the Seymour sisters' poem also directly challenges Elizabeth's translation by splitting apart the directives of queenship and mothering, taking out of the vernacular the laws of motherhood and rewriting how female power is transmitted, affection rewarded, and families reproduced.

Chapter 2, "Borrowed Robes," explores the newly crowned Elizabeth's decision to wear her sister Mary's robes to her own 1559 coronation. To be sure, such a recycling of royal garments made political and economic sense, since clothes were precious commodities and sovereign robes were seen to retain much of the authority they ceremonially conferred. But I also read Elizabeth's borrowing as evidence about the value of maternal legacies in early modern England, drawing on the work of anthropologists who describe cloth's usefulness in the "reproduction" of mothering, along with the researches of costume historians who describe the common early modern practice of "trauncelating" women's garments. As Ann Rosalind Jones and Peter Stallybrass put it, early modern women's vestments also functioned as material investments, yet the many mothers' advice books produced at this time—including popular works by Elizabeth Clinton, Dorothy Leigh,

10 *Women's Wealth and Women's Writing in Early Modern England*

and Elizabeth Jocelin, whose 1622 tract describes the "little legacy" she leaves behind for her husband and child[20]—uncover other ways that women's property might circulate. I argue that these writings similarly center on the importance and fungibility of maternal ties, outlining ways that a mother's authority might be confidently appropriated or, like Mary Tudor's dress, easily remade.

In Chapter 3, "Manifest Housekeepers," I explore the corpus of needlework and poetry produced by Elizabeth Tudor's cousin and political rival Mary Stuart during nearly twenty years of confinement under the English queen. Indeed, for most of her adult life, Mary's private world was spent under lock and key, but her imprisonment also provided a venue for ambition, espionage, and intrigue. The texts and cloth Mary fashions during her long captivity reflect both the wealth and poverty of this strange "domestic space," supplying an equivocal portrait of queenly retirement and maternal solicitude, with elaborate skirts for her cousin assembled alongside treasonous bed cushions forwarded to Mary's supporters in the Catholic North.[21] Mary's poetry and letters similarly display a complex pattern of threats and retreats, abandonment and affection. Her long-questioned love sonnets, reportedly uncovered by English authorities during Mary's trial, similarly represent Mary's power and her powerlessness, outlining the image of a queen whose capacity to rule is tied up with her ability to forswear it.

Chapter 4, "Strange Bedfellows," centers on another royal claimant and long-term prisoner, Mary Stuart's niece Arbella. My focus is on the unusual collection of letters Arbella produces during her ten years of confinement at her grandmother Bess of Hardwick's estate. Cut off from the courtly life for which she had been carefully groomed, Arbella's letters are written under harsh conditions of isolation and deprivation. In these writings, she brazenly plots her escape, transacts treasonous marriage plans with another royal claimant, and outlandishly describes an affair with the King of Scots as a way to throw off Elizabeth's investigators. The effect—reminiscent of Mary Stuart's extravagant productions—is to transform the household prison into a site of sovereign autonomy and imperial fantasy, and to recreate herself as a valuable household object of desire. The threat Arbella posed to her Queen has been taken more seriously in the last twenty years, but I concentrate on the letters' confounding designs as evidence of a drastically altered conception of female wealth and influence.[22] Presenting herself as rival to her Queen and lover of Elizabeth's successor, Stuart's letters—however fictive or unreliable—tell us much about changing ideas of female authority, kinship, and subordination, and suggest how female subjects might now strive to manage their interests and ambitions in the absence of a larger women's world.

My fifth chapter, "Girles aflote," explores Arbella Stuart's 1610 sale of the

---

[20] See Sylvia Brown (1999, p. 106).

[21] The most useful and detailed discussion of Mary's needlework and its charged political messages remains that of Swain (1973).

[22] Steen (*Letters*, 1994) and Gristwood both read Arbella's letters in light of the aging Elizabeth's own paranoia.

needlework panels that her grandmother and Mary Stuart had jointly produced nearly forty years earlier. In this instance, Stuart was not only trading an heirloom for hard cash, but also signaling a disruption in the world of women that had long surrounded her. As a husbandless, orphaned young woman—not unlike the Cordelia or Perdita whom Shakespeare imagines in his late plays—Stuart supplies a clear example of the poverty and abjection many single women felt in a world less animated by gifts, more centered around consumer goods. This is a world that contemporary poets Amelilia Lanyer and Isabella Whitney investigate as well. Whitney's poetry in particular outlines a similar situation of isolation and renunciation in a changing world of property, kin, and affection, where things were not shared but given away. I explore Bess of Hardwick's later career in light of this changing world as well, for the widowed Bess's efforts likewise increasingly center around inventories of material goods. Landowner and merchant, wife, mother, prolific needlewoman and confidant of two queens, Bess amasses a huge fortune during her long life and spends her last years combining the tasks of mothering with those of a magnate, her writings organized by the legal and moral language of the will.

Throughout these five chapters, I also explore what happens to the complicated figure and ambitions of the woman writer, the multifaceted shape of her audience and provenance of her work inside and outside the household, working with the premise that any theory of women's literary production at this time needs to take into account what relates women to each other. Virginia Woolf had raised the same kind of connection nearly a century ago. Describing a nascent female literary tradition gradually taking shape in the eighteenth century, she obliquely pointed to some of these powerful female ties, claiming that "we think back through our mothers if we are women" (p. 76), but also imagining maternal labors as continually thwarted, often stillborn. Woolf's picture is a limited one, however. The early modern woman who writes is not struggling to write, at least in the pictures Bess and Elizabeth, Mary and Arbella offer to us, and their "little legacies' are immense ones, for what they copied or stitched or traded or otherwise exchanged with each other is also at the center of courtly politics, the succession crisis, religious reform, and the increasingly private shape of domestic life. By tracing what early some modern women might expect to inherit from, share with, or bequest to each other, I also hope to establish who might possess maternal influence, how a mother's powers might be wielded or reproduced, and what, ultimately, these powers might shape.

Chapter 1
Miroir or Glasse

I am not only bound to serve you but also to revere you with daughterly love.[1]

Although I could not be plentiful in giving thanks for the manifold kindness received at your highness' hand at my departure, yet I am something to be borne withal.[2]

A page from the school notebook of fifteen-year-old Rachel Fane (1613?–1680), granddaughter of Grace, Lady Mildmay, dutifully lists a number of injunctions for modesty and moderation, admonishing those who sleep or drink too much, who "rashly plight thy troth," or who neglect to hide their parents' "weakenesse."[3] Fane's work is a carefully produced transcription of Cato, English versions of which were popular in both early modern homes and schools, but these schoolgirl exercises also supply clear testimony of a young girl's mature concerns, especially regarding the proper, patient treatment of her parents, whose "errer [might] make them swarve aside." Such exercises were frequently designed for the daughters of nobles and gentry to foster morality and handwriting as well as to advertise to marriageability or learning, but they might also demonstrate how these attributes were simultaneously tied up with the exacting project of being a daughter: learning without rebellion, ambition that had no real intellectual outlet, precision and rigor put entirely at the service of one's betters, all pieces of an unusually pliable form of knowledge that could go underground or stay unmoored from any clear sense of the self. Such aims are confidently outlined in schoolmaster Thomas Salter's 1579 educational treatise. "[W]ho can doubt," Salter reasons, "the accomplishment of a maiden who, by virtuous instruction and ample evidence, has learned to govern a household wisely?"[4] Little wonder that "daughterly love" and thanks, as Princess Elizabeth notes in letters to her stepmother Katherine Parr (excerpted above), might adhere to rather conventional boundaries or respect such obvious limits.

Upper class girls were often educated at home or in the households of other noble families, but the early modern schools for wealthy daughters that we know about, typically run by married women and situated in London neighborhoods,

---

[1] A letter from Elizabeth to Katherine Parr, dated July 31, 1544 (*Collected Works* 5).

[2] Elizabeth's letter to Parr after Parr sends her away in May 1548. Quoted by James 323.

[3] See the anthology edited by Ostovich and Sauer; Fane's work is discussed by Bowden (pp. 74–7). Elsewhere, Bowden (2004) discusses Fane's translation of Cato and explores Fane's other writings comprising a collection of twelve notebooks, including a masque and other entertainments, musical arrangements, and recipes (pp. 166–7).

[4] Quoted by Holm (p. 210).

appear likewise designed to educate daughters in "certain accomplishments of polite society" (Yeandle, p. 272). We have a seventeenth-century description of one of these schools, a boarding and day school in Windsor for daughters of ladies and gentlewomen where, as Laetitia Yeandle reports, the education of girls included "[needle]worke, reading, writing, and dancing—as well as, for an additional eight pounds, music and singing (p. 273). Obviously aristocratic impulses to educate daughters could be economic or moralistic, loving or controlling; and these different motives could work together, even if they did not run very deep. Their range is explored by Janis Butler Holm, who includes religious education, humanist values, and training for wifely duties as informing the education of young women. Holm also points out that other scholars have frequently ignored the ambivalence surrounding the education of daughters, clinging instead to a "myth of a feminist humanism" (p.197). She makes pointed reference to Salter's treatise, which ironically discourages its female readers from the study of liberal arts, condemns "the light or vaine glorie of learnyng," and emphasizes instead the virtues and behaviors associated with domestic conduct, particularly with the care of a husband, children, and those tasks that would increasingly define the role of the early modern housewife. Allowing the female child to "be present at all things pertaining to household affairs, for her early experience," Salter advises, "will persuade others of her promise as an expert housewife."[5]

There seems little reason, then, to look too closely at the work of daughters, except as evidence about the pressures, influences, and intentions that they had to absorb or reflect. Edmund Spenser's schoolmaster Richard Mulcaster carefully outlines this analogy in his 1581 *Positions*, claiming that since women's employment "is within limit, . . . so must their traine be."[6] Yet sometimes we find daughters exploring their ties to people and things in unusual detail and care in their writing exercises or embroidered samplers or still more ambitious undertakings. Imitating her mother or another woman could provide a young girl with the means of discovering herself as an agent or as an author—someone who creates value and shares meaning in the world of women—such that household duties could serve as powerful instruments of affiliation and identification or even, as Fane's notebook carefully suggests, of loyal and measured opposition.

If we find some of the same circumscribed pedagogy illustrated in the needlework produced extensively by young girls in the early modern period, we should likewise appreciate how these efforts were designed to give shape to a daughter's impulses, memories, lessons, and ideas.[7] Lanto Synge tells us, for instance, that on small lengths of cloth, an industrious, bored, or simply precocious young girl might record examples of stitches, border patterns, and motifs in "a

---

[5]   See Holm (pp. 201, 212). Cf. Michalove, who argues that although aristocratic women did not typically receive formal training in the humanities, they, like women from all classes, "were educated for the positions they would hold in society" (p. 69).

[6]   Quoted by Snook (p. 11).

[7]   See studies by Ring and Synge.

Fig. 1.1   Jane Bostocke's 1598 sampler, exhibiting a range of patterns, letters, and stitches, and advertising a daughter's ingenuity alongside her ability to conform.

kind of notebook" "always at hand" (p. 82). Rarely did such efforts result in something larger or more coherent, at least to most observers' eyes; Susan Frye (2000) describes them, for instance, as "fragments of literacy" rather than as more successful and complete artifacts (pp. 224–5). But even the most conventional, formulaic efforts of juvenile hands could permit a daughter's construction of

16   *Women's Wealth and Women's Writing in Early Modern England*

herself in relation to others, especially to her mother, as well as in relation to other plans or ambitions or fears she might herself hold.

Indeed, a larger motive or more coherent framework—and some explanation for the attention daughters frequently lavished upon their efforts—starts to emerge once we think about the many different roles of mothers in these works, as teachers, models, recipients, readers, sources, or subjects of inquiry. Other critics have suggested the importance of this maternal context in women's work; as Frye suggests, "[f]rom the earliest publications by women in the sixteenth century to those of the seventeenth century, women authors wrote from the subject position of daughter, mother, wife, and widow whether they married or not, had children or not."[8] Frye's is a contentious claim because of the assumptions it makes about demographics and economics, skirting the numbers which suggest that nearly half of the female population in the seventeenth century was widowed or never-married (see Froide, pp.236–7). Nonetheless, there are a number of issues at work in Frye's picture of "maternal textuality" that asks us to acknowledge the ways that mothers—understood at once and, sometimes at odds, as nurturers, rivals, wives, origins, benefactors—figure so prominently in many women's works, even in the projects of translation or handwriting or needlework that younger hands might undertake.

Especially noteworthy is the way that many works of daughters subtly direct energies to the project of shaping mothers and apportioning their influence, devising an intellectual program or spiritual pedigree that had little to do either with marriageability or with decorum and more with the aim of establishing or furthering a useful tie to some other woman. As Princess Elizabeth writes in a letter accompanying the 1544 New Year's gift, "[T]he seal of your excellent wit and godly learning in the reading of it . . . shall rub out, polish, and mend" any errors in the work.[9] The tie between these women seems particularly useful because it is at once intimate and official—reinforced, too, by household tasks of mending and polishing—sidestepping fathers and husbands while bridging "manual" or material concerns with spiritual and political needs. The relationship is transforming as well, creating a debt by presenting a gift and invoking the recipient as an author, patron, teacher, and fellow servant.

Such a transformation of female subjects and their objects is a common one. Indeed, any account of early modern women's work needs to include the facts that it is often conventional and collaborative, related to the demands of kin or the household (whatever its size) and involving, as a result, a "translation" of some

---

[8]   Frye (2000), p. 234. For another view, see Heale, who argues, "In moving into print, the role of woman as crucial to the production of courtly verse disappeared from sight" (pp. 31, 26).

[9]   This, and all other excerpts from Elizabeth's translation of Marguerite de Navarre's religious poem, is taken from the edition prepared by Shell (p. 12). Hereafter, all excerpts will be noted parenthetically in the text. See also the reading of this dedication provided by Quilligan (2005), pp. 48–9.

Miroir or Glasse

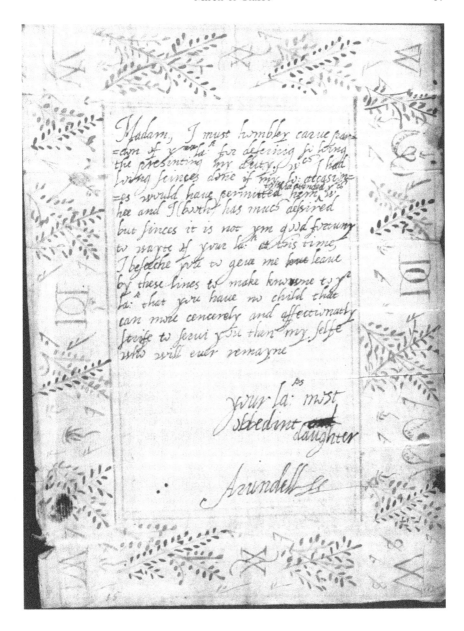

Fig. 1.2 Letter Alathea Talbot Howard, Countess of Arundell, to her grandmother Bess of Hardwick. The letter is designed to look like a sampler, making a gift out of an inventory of a granddaughter's duties.

other woman's efforts or productions; such work, in other words, is best explained by what relates women to each other. Dympna Callaghan emphasizes the material nature of this work rather than its collaborative nature, two features which, I think, really belong together. This much is suggested when Callaghan argues that "in the early modern context, much women's 'writing' includes ditties, rhymes, and prayers that have specific and practical uses in the everyday world and as such probably have more in common with material artifacts than with literature per se" (p. 54).

The numerous letters addressed to Bess of Hardwick from daughters and granddaughters, for instance, exploit the material properties and assumptions of "daughterly love," weighing economic and moral claims by calculating debts, favors, and what Bess's granddaughter Alathea Talbot Howard (probably aged twenty-five at the time) coolly terms "the presenting of my duty." In a beautifully prepared letter, drafted sometime between 1606 and Bess's death in 1608, Alathea transforms a familial responsibility into a lavish object in the same way that her elaborately decorated note, drafted in apology for "deferring" this duty "so long," rewrites the power and intentions governing their tie. At once a rejection of conventional gift-giving and a valuable gift in itself, Alathea's letter is actually fashioned to resemble a schoolgirl sampler with the borders drawn to look like stitches: its display of technique is a sign of steady devotion, political calculation, and artistic vision. Later chapters will explore more fully the ways such objects produced by and shared between women substantiate, and even substitute for, kin ties by linking moral with material identity; my concern here, though, is on the ways gifts transform daughters into authors by endowing mothers with history and with property.[10]

Women's worlds were busy and rich with a constant flow of things and people in and out of households, and a daughter might attribute different things to the many women who had overseen her development, her debts ones that gifts of identification, forgiveness, or recollection might indicate or try to obscure. Even her love for a father (or for her mother's husband) could signify loyalty or disloyalty; marrying well might advance her mother's economic interests or divide her from them; and becoming herself a mother, as Nancy Chodorow has argued, might either replicate a mother's love or somehow repair its damages. Being a daughter was a closely regulated—even calibrated—position, especially in the social world of the early modern aristocratic family, its cares and rewards often governed from without, its challenges and satisfactions regularly meted out by whatever material terms were demanded by devotion, fear, loyalty, or ambition. Identification of interests could create mothers and daughters more powerfully than any physiology. Lady Anne Clifford will labor, under her mother's constant approval and encouragement, to wage war against her father's estate with the help

---

[10] For an account of the sixteenth-century housewife's twinned moral and material responsibilities, see Ajmar, (p. 83). Ajmar focuses on domestic space and domestic objects, and she argues that "the rise in status of domestic objects associated with women and the status of women themselves went hand in hand" (p. 76).

of the king and lawyers and early modern courts as a way, for instance, to claim her share of her father's patrimony as his only direct heir. But other daughters' efforts might aim instead to reclaim mothers or rescue them from seclusion, slander, damnation or self-pity, to set them loose in the world or at the throne of Christ in heaven. Princess Elizabeth endows her efforts with this divine purpose in her New Year's gift, elevating herself through affection for a king's wife, exclaiming, "Who did ever hear speak of such a thing as to raise up one so high which of herself was nothing, and maketh of a great value this that of itself was naught[?]" (Shell, p. 131).

***

The earliest productions of Elizabeth Tudor—a handful of letters, translations, prayers, poems, and needlework—are often studied as the rather conventional results of a privileged childhood, without much investigation into the kind of time, knowledge, intimacy and need they display, or what they demand of their audience (the instructions to Parr accompanying the New Year's gift, for example, not only include a request for corrections but also the hope that Parr will keep the work private). Gifts prepared by the princess and distributed to her stepmother–like ones presented to her father and brother during the same period–are evidence of considerable learning and piety, critics agree, but seem to possess less merit as literary works.[11] Such an evaluation, however, overlooks what so much of women's efforts–literary and otherwise–were designed to accomplish in the early modern period, especially the degree to which they served as objects to be presented to or exchanged with other women who knew how to read the meanings these works carefully and, sometimes, lovingly encoded. The eleven-year-old Elizabeth's gift to Parr, a hand-copied prose translation of Marguerite de Navarre's religious poem *Miroir de l ame Pecheresse* (1531) entitled *The Miroir or Glasse of the Synneful Soul*, is especially noteworthy as a work exploring the powers and vagaries of female ties, particularly those between children and parents, princesses and queens.[12]

The tie between Elizabeth and Katherine remained inordinately close if painfully awkward in the years to come, when the fifteen-year-old Elizabeth reportedly had an affair with Thomas Seymour. Henry's widow had secretly married Seymour in 1547, after the death of the king just months before.[13] Parr

---

[11]   For a discussion of the ways Elizabeth's academic training provided by Roger Ascham contradicted the pedagogy of her sister Mary's tutor Juan Luis Vives, see Vosevich, who writes: "These opposing pedagogies produced very different Tudor rulers: Mary, who fashioned herself a 'princess' or 'queen;' and Elizabeth, who preferred 'prince' or 'king'"(p. 62). Mary, accordingly, did not publish her translation of Erasmus (p. 65).

[12]   Beilin offers an overview of Marguerite's poem and Elizabeth's translation (pp. 67–72). See also Prescott's discussion (pp. 73–4). Nevanlinna compares Elizabeth's poem with the version published three years later by John Bale. For the claim that women rulers like Elizabeth and Catherine de Medici knew "their shared royal female prerogatives depended, to some degree on the achievements of each other," see Quilligan (2006, para 4).

[13]   James (1999) offers details (pp. 320–32); see also Cavanagh (pp. 9–10).

had been instrumental in restoring Elizabeth and Mary to the succession, so this tie carried heavy dynastic and political weight: in winning her stepmother's affection, Elizabeth could also be safeguarding a hard-won political position. The two women's charged connection continued to require the scrutiny of the state, as we will see; but it also demanded the labors of another set of daughters to set it aright. In 1550, the three oldest daughters of Edward Seymour (1506–1562) take up the project Elizabeth had apparently driven aground, reworking and clarifying the princess's ideas about maternal lines and female influence in a poem the sisters jointly compose. These young girls were, like Elizabeth, impressively learned, and their connections to Edward VI's court not unlike those of the princess. Thomas Seymour's elder brother Edward would rule as lord protector of England during Edward VI's brief reign. A "Reformation intellectual and politician," Edward Seymour's tremendous, even ruthless political ambition must be viewed, Patricia Demers maintains, alongside his deep and learned piety.[14] Seymour's second wife Anne Stanhope (1497–1587) was extremely influential in her own right, too, as a lady-in-waiting to Parr and important patron of Reformist scholars and authors. Stanhope took enormous pains to find tutors for her children, and one of these tutors probably encouraged daughters Margaret (ca. 1534–?), Jane (1541–1560), and Anne Seymour (ca. 1532–1587) to collaborate on a long poem in Latin, even though the youngest member of this group was only nine years old at the time.

The Seymour sisters' impressive efforts were quickly recognized across the continent when their tutor (possibly a Huguenot spy) had the hundred and four distichs published. Whether the poem served as public evidence of the daughters' marriageability or of their parents' reformist sympathies, the *Hecatodistichon* (1550, reprinted 1551) also revises the awkward, albeit intimate, picture of sovereign connections that Princess Elizabeth had drafted six years previously, even if the Seymours never mention, either directly or indirectly, Elizabeth's work.

The later history of the Seymour sisters is brief and shadowy. We know that Anne married, but many sources support rumors of her insanity in middle age; Jane died at 19, a Lady of the Bedchamber at Elizabeth's court; and Margaret predeceased Jane.[15] Yet the literary contribution of these young women is exceptional and important, utterly commanding in its picture of three sisters drawing on collected resources of faith, wisdom, and metrics. Brenda Hosington (1996) reminds us of their work's strangeness and value in remarking that the *Hecatodistichon* was "the first formal and original verse encomium in Latin written by a female author to be printed in England" (p. 163). Collectively undertaken to commemorate the death of Marguerite de Navarre one year earlier, the *Hecatodistichon* takes for its subject the strange and elusive image of the Queen of Navarre as ghost, sibling, mother, and queen—the very same dim and shifting presence that Elizabeth, in translating

---

[14] See Demers pp. (345–7). Demers's essay includes an edited version of the sisters' poem, which I will draw on and cite parenthetically in the text.

[15] Beilin offers some information about the Seymour sisters (p. 179); for additional details, see Hosington (1996) and the introductory notes to her 2000 edition.

Marguerite's work, had tried to make sense of only a few years before. Like Fane's loving explorations of authority and submission, both of these works register the tricky politics involved in being a daughter, sometimes even putting that biological position into doubt; indeed, that female ties are awkward, possibly fictive, and forceful only because they are metaphorical is a central theme.[16] Elizabeth's *Glasse* and the Seymours' *Hecatodistichon* are centered on but not directed to the sovereign maternal figure Marguerite had presented in her 1531 poem, an extended meditation in rhyming couplets casting the author as daughter, mother, sister, and wife of Christ. Marguerite's poem was reissued several times, although it had been briefly condemned by the Sorbonne at its initial appearance, probably because of the way the author dispenses with the sacraments and clergy in favor of God's sheer love for the faithless sinner.[17] The spiritual journey Marguerite's speaker describes is fantastic and wildly successful, spanning an ascent from self-loathing to acceptance, hell to heavenly bliss, violation and despair to forgiveness and absorption, and isolated anguish to communion with God who is husband, father, brother, and son.

Marguerite's figure of heavenly reward in terms of powerful kin ties, in turn, apparently enabled four aristocratic girls the chance not to see themselves as queens, marriageable maidens, or potential mothers of kings, but as daughters and sisters who inhabit a sovereign cosmos through the pull of gratitude and affection rather than through rank or influence or wealth. Still, all four refuse to emulate Marguerite's rather easy acceptance of the role of the beloved (see Prescott, p. 64) and their revisions to Marguerite's picture, if subtle, are extensive, as I will explore more fully later. There are a number of images of ambivalent and inimical maternal figures in many literary works of the period, to be sure. The fruitless reign of Elizabeth herself is ultimately the most famous, but such a conflicted, even forbidding, maternal presence looms in the muted advice bestowed in countless mother's manuals (explored more fully in Chapter 2), as well as in the disappearance and stony reappearance of Shakespeare's Hermione or his picture of Cleopatra suckling an asp, or in the series of warring maternal figures in Elizabeth Cary's 1613 *Tragedy of Mariam*.[18] In these two texts a similar tension is at work, for just as Marguerite's legacy to Elizabeth is transformed by the princess's debts to her stepmother, the Seymours' obvious borrowings from Elizabeth are translated into an elegy for her source: the affiliations are as powerful as they are circumvented, as if kinship ties can be edited.

The elaborate gestures of four daughters to rescue mothers from shame or poverty or sin will be intimately tied to Elizabethan politics in the years that follow, too. Parliament's many pleas for Elizabeth to marry and produce an heir are one long-standing example of an early modern project to create and adjust maternal

---

[16]   Quilligan (2005) likewise describes the "endogamous focus" of Elizabeth's *Glasse* (p. 48).

[17]   Publication history is offered by Demers (p. 350) and Prescott (p. 62).

[18]   I am indebted here to Skura's reading of Cary's play.

ties, but Protestant doctrines that repudiated the Virgin Mary and emptied out convents are another. What we see, however, in the early efforts of daughters like Elizabeth Tudor and Anne, Margaret, and Jane Seymour, however, is something even more ambitious, articulating both a vision of kinship as supplying *all* of the economic, political, and psychological demands of a lifetime, and of a maternal figure endowed with incredible knowledge and authority, once she's been freed from the constraints of her family.

***

Erin Murphy suggests that many early modern writers saw in the family a form to impose on cultural wishes about history, power, sex, blame, and regeneration— on ideas, perhaps, about what a good daughter could accomplish.[19] Milton's Eve is the most famous example, as Murphy expertly details, at once an incestuous daughter and mother sinfully attempting to claim power from the father. Other authors find ways to give ambitious maternal figures the means to succeed. One method, employed both by Elizabeth and the Seymour sisters, involves rebuilding maternal genealogy, dividing mothers from their progeny, for instance, or emphasizing gender at the expense of sexuality. A similar reckoning of maternal powers and limits is at work in their source, as we see when Marguerite's *Miroir* provides an exegesis of the biblical story of King Solomon presiding over a conflict between two mothers, both of whom claim the same living child (1 Kings 3). Whereas Marguerite emphasizes the mothers' debate over a dead child, her literary descendants focus instead upon the faulty shape that mothering can assume, either through carelessness or inattention, criminality or mere ignorance (see Shell, p. 123). The attachment to mothers can be one-sided, and Margaret Seymour raises this danger as a grave political one, musing in the *Hecatodistichon*: "Now that the Queen has left the court, what next?" (see Demers, line 47).

The choice of Marguerite as a predecessor was a loaded one at this time, in any case. Sister of the French king Francois I, Marguerite, Queen of Navarre (1492–1549), was famed in European courtly circles for her letters and learning, piety and wit, patronage and royal influence with kings, Elizabeth Tudor's father among them.[20] Anne Boleyn had briefly been in Marguerite's service in the 1520s, and both women were apparently contenders for Henry's hand, for there was at least some discussion of Marguerite's marriage to Henry when he was seeking a divorce from Catherine of Aragon, Marguerite being similarly reform-minded although officially a Catholic. Elizabeth may be testing the possibility of other mothers in

---

[19] See Murphy's unpublished paper, "Copulating with the Mother: *Paradise Lost* and the Politics of Begetting."

[20] As Brown (2004) argues, "Marguerite of Navarre herself functions in varied ways in Renaissance culture . . . her text and Elizabeth's *Glass* all underwent a retrospective process of radicalization in the sixteenth century" (p. 93). Brown also notes the irony that "a Roman Catholic French tract . . . plays a part in the constitution of the Protestant English nation" (p. 94).

Fig. 1.3 The upper cover and binding embroidered by Princess Elizabeth for *The Glasse*. A silver knot pattern is used for Katherine's initials and the pansies. Like Alathea Howard's letter, embroidery and literacy not only reinforce but duplicate each other in a daughter's work.

24   *Women's Wealth and Women's Writing in Early Modern England*

her translation, but her choice of Marguerite as an influence was something many Protestant authors did in their early efforts to establish a spiritual pedigree.[21] Elizabeth's translation, the first English edition of Marguerite's long poem, is beautifully rendered in italic hand on paper, Margaret Swain observes, "faintly ruled into fourteen lines to keep the pages evenly spaced."[22] The front and back covers were also embroidered by the princess, and in the center of each cover are Parr's interlaced initials. The princess's careful needlework is consistent with descriptions of other early modern daughters' samplers, which frequently employed a simple chain stitch, here worked in gold and silver wire with blue silk.[23] In fact, Jennifer Summit's treatment (2000) of this artifact reads in its limited circuit a limited ambition. "From childhood Elizabeth produced texts within predominantly female, household space," she says, although Summit views the adult career as making use of the same limits for political gain: "As a queen, Elizabeth continued to produce and circulate texts that created intimate networks among women" (pp. 168, 170). In contrast, Georgia E. Brown reads a radical ambition in the princess's undertaking, describing the "community of female authors who inspire" Elizabeth's text: "Elizabeth's Glass inscribes the princess within a community of reform-minded, royal authoresses, privileging matrilineage over patrilineage, spiritual and intellectual inheritance over inheritance of the blood, and constructs a collaborative model of reading and writing" (p. 96).

My interpretation falls somewhere in between, because I am more convinced of Elizabeth's efforts at outreach than of their success. But whether we see Elizabeth's artistry as eventually serving more important political aims or as *always* concerning itself with the genealogy of royal power, we need to be careful about any untroubled association between female networks and household space; in the case of Marguerite and Elizabeth, both sisters of kings, their writings doubly wield and implore power, and that is their point: they have an interest in manipulating things at court from without, Princess Elizabeth shrewdly protecting her designs by presenting them to such a trusted and powerful yet similarly vulnerable friend, whose own religious sympathies would arouse a king's suspicions. Still, even though the princess's translation was later amended (probably by one of her tutors) and then published abroad by Bale in 1548 (and then reprinted at least four more times during her long reign), we ought to see this work as profoundly intimate and, as Maureen Quilligan (2005) claims, *inalienable*, remaining linked to Elizabeth, however closely it follows Marguerite's text (p. 48). As the princess writes to Parr

---

[21]   Both Summit (2000) and Snook (pp. 34–44) comment on the Protestant publication of Anne Askew's writings with this aim. Summit, in particular, describes the efforts of Protestant reformers like John Bale to find in the woman writer a potent figure of Catholic opposition, embodying in her very marginality and simplicity (or immaturity, in Elizabeth's case) a nascent vernacular tradition (pp. 110–13).

[22]   Swain, "A New Year's Gift" (1973), p. 260.

[23]   See Synge's discussion of samplers (pp. 82–5); additional details about Elizabeth's handiwork are offered by Klein (1997) and Quilligan (2000).

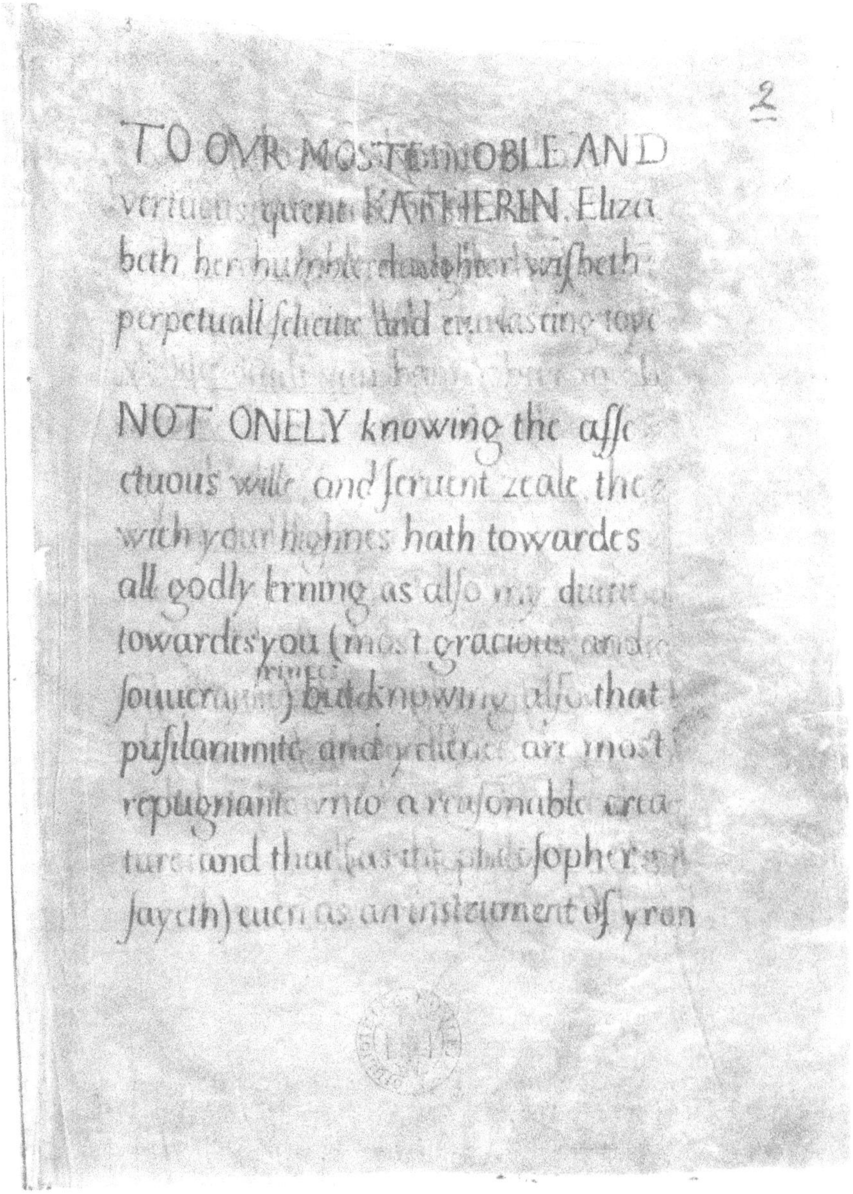

Fig. 1.4   Elizabeth's dedication of *The Glasse* to her stepmother Katherine Parr. The lined text, careful print, and pointed address to her teacher would, a century later, mark the schoolgirl's sampler.

in the letter that accompanies her gift, her poem is also a mirror or glass in which Elizabeth might better see herself, "beholding and contemplating what she is" (Shell, p. 111).

This mirroring effect continues in the translation which follows, only here, the rewards of self-scrutiny are outlined, too. "All her treasures," the princess suggests, "are nothing else but sins which Thou hast taken upon Thee, and paid all her whole debt":

> With Thy goods and great lands, Thou hast made her so rich, and with so great a jointure, that she (knowing herself to be Thy avowed wife) doth believe to be quit of all that she oweth, esteeming very little that she doth see here beneath. She forsaketh her old father, and all the goods that he giveth, for her husband's sake. (Shell, p. 119)

The *Glasse* is magical, too, doing away with fathers by transforming poor and sinful daughters into dutiful and wealthy wives. There are, however, rough edges to Elizabeth's picture of mothering and places where Henry's cruel charges against her mother are repeated. In the economy which Marguerite had outlined, mothers have and renounce wealth: they are also close readers, dedicated scholars, and holders of secrets. But Elizabeth's translation describes these same mothers as "naughty wom[e]n" (Shell, p. 120), adulterous and unashamed, lewd and unworthy of a husband's healing love or of an "old father's" vast goods.

***

Two of the most attentive readers of Elizabeth's *Glasse*, Marc Shell and Anne Lake Prescott, treat the translation's weaknesses and missteps as keys to the childish thinking and longings that animated the princess's efforts. Prescott, for instance, comments on Elizabeth's literal-mindedness as well as on the way she flattens Marguerite's ardent, even erotic language in describing the soul's newfound intimacy with God (p. 68). The immaturity or awkwardness suggests itself in other ways, too. As Prescott comments, "the absence of any reference to the Queen of Navarre is quite puzzling in a manuscript presented to the English queen while the French author was enjoying renewed importance" (p. 71). One might read in such errors Elizabeth's cloudy sense of the rumors surrounding her mother, her father's cruelty and her bastardy, but Prescott finds in them testimony about a child's more basic fears of abandonment, arguing that "Elizabeth had come to feel within her very marrow the pain and ambiguity of family ties. Interestingly, poignantly, her relatively few errors and her somewhat more frequent omissions often concern this set of relationships" (p. 68). Little wonder that Elizabeth's text lingers over the promise of adoption, with praise of God as a divine home-wrecker who "hast broken the kindred of my old father" (Shell, p. 121) and who rewards goodly women with reinvigorated kin ties. As Elizabeth puts it in the letter accompanying her gift, "how of herself and of her own strength she can do nothing that good is, or prevaileth for her salvation, unless it be through the grace of God, whose mother, daughter, sister, and wife by the scriptures she proveth herself to be" (Shell, p. 111).

With these pressing personal aims in mind, Frances Teague maintains that to assess Elizabeth's work only as a translation is to misread it: "[T]he actual value lies in its associations" (p. 35). Actually, metaphors of kinship are not as much relied upon in Elizabeth's translation as they are continually tested. "O what conjunction," the princess exclaims, musing over God's powers to reclaim and renew her (Shell, p. 133); elsewhere, she asks whether "there [is] any father to the daughter, or else brother to the sister, which would ever do as He hath done[?]" (Shell, p. 117). The Seymour sisters, as we will see, do not test kinship metaphors but stretch them, making them interchangeable and thereby letting them carry vast theological, political, and epistemological weight. But Elizabeth carefully respects their limits and sometimes she even divides these ties, taking enormous pains to elucidate the worlds of pain and affection between them. Elizabeth's caution has some surprising effects, for it sometimes allows her to assume power and discharge debts to her betters: "Now, my Lord, if Thou be my father, may I think that I am Thy mother?" (Shell, p. 119).

Valerie Wayne helps us better understand the early modern "authorisation of motherhood" that Elizabeth's translation tentatively explores, a transformation more explicitly documented by a spate of advice books for women produced in the seventeenth century (p. 60). Acknowledging that motherhood has a complicated history, however, also means recognizing that it might be supported by different things at different times, including a range of emotions, political and economic resources, religious meanings, and social values. Elizabeth's gift to Parr affirms their tie and her stepmother's influence with Henry, but it also suggests how limited or uncertain those powers are, even how unnecessary, given God's grace and the fact that mothering is *always* metaphorical, always premised on promises. Ultimately, their tie becomes irrelevant as well: Parr will die at 36 after giving birth to a daughter of her own, and Elizabeth will assume the throne herself ten years later, unmarried, childless, carefully manipulating (and occasionally manufacturing) a knowing, loving world of kin (see Orlin, 1995).

***

That Elizabeth's depiction of herself in the *Miroir or Glasse* as Katherine's student and grateful child should be viewed as a literary project with debts to other mothers is suggested by the Seymour sisters' elegy for Marguerite de Navarre, published on the continent in 1551. Cousins to Edward VI, their little-known collaboration was widely praised at the time as a rare instance of female piety and learning. But the *Hecatodistichon* can also be seen as a response to Elizabeth's earlier evocation of Marguerite, her relationship to Parr, and her uneasy tie to a dead mother. The *Hecatodistichon* translates what Elizabeth makes of Marguerite's image, preserving this mother's memory by formally casting her out.

Like Elizabeth's *Glasse*, the *Hecatodistichon* is composed by daughters of marriageable age during a period when they would typically be expected to leave their mothers for father-figure spouses. One motive behind these "schoolgirl exercises" may thus be to make the mother tie as fungible as the paternal tie, so as to exchange mother or father figures with more confidence or ease. The painful complications surrounding this remodeling of maternal power are envisioned by the Seymours in terms of a conflict between being God's lovesick bride and a mother's dutiful daughter. Naomi Scheman explains how a daughter experiences the demands of each role as rival ones, describing the maturation of female desire and subjectivity as occurring "within the systems of male privilege [whereby] neither her appropriately feminine sexual identity nor her ability to assume public power is compatible with her being her mother's daughter."[24] But what if one could remain one's mother's daughter through all of the vicissitudes of eros and politics, the whims of kings and humiliation of fathers? The rewards, at least for Elizabeth, could be profound, permitting her to somehow obscure her father's ill wishes or political disfavor, even his constant neglect.

Instead, Elizabeth is orphaned at 14, and after Henry's death, the fortunes of Elizabeth and the Seymour sisters are strangely reversed. Edward Seymour assumes the position of lord protector, ruling in Elizabeth's nine-year-old brother's stead. Seymour orders Katherine Parr, unmentioned in Henry's will, to return her gifts of jewelry to the crown, and Seymour redistributes them to his wife.[25] Retha Warnicke has investigated popular contemporary parallels between the Seymours' mother and Anne Boleyn as wicked women meddling in affairs of state and seducing statesmen, but Warnicke also notes that Stanhope was a prominent literary patron who attended several queens and would later even care for Parr's infant daughter. Just as Parr's household was a center for Protestant learning and reform, Stanhope presided over a small but influential collection of reformist scholars, tutors, and spies.[26] The connections between the two households multiply still further when the dowager queen Parr, with the Princess Elizabeth as part of her household, married Seymour's brother just months after Henry's death, and only a short time after Thomas Seymour's reported marital designs on the princess were rejected by the lord protector.

Gossip about her new husband and stepdaughter continues, and during Twelfth Night festivities in January 1548, the pregnant Parr reputedly finds the two in each other's arms, although Elizabeth was not sent away until months later, when Parr's period of confinement approached. Parr dies in September 1548, a few days after the birth of a daughter. In the midst of the allegations surrounding Elizabeth, the ascent of Anne Stanhope, the birth of Parr's daughter Mary, and Marguerite's death, the Seymours embark on a recovery project of their own, signaling once more the importance of the maternal bond, now an unusually sensitive register of

---

[24] Scheman (p. 136). Scheman also cites Flax's exploration of the daughter's need to rescue her mother.

[25] Warnicke (pp. 25–6). Professor Warnicke generously provided me with a copy of this essay.

[26] See King for additional details about Parr and Stanhope's households (p. 53).

all the turmoil at court—and also detailing how a good daughter might achieve both heaven and earth at home.[27]

The *Hecatodistichon* provides clear evidence of the first-rate education of aristocratic daughters as well as of the kinds of marriages they might hope to transact through such a pious Protestant offering. Patricia Demers suggests that "[t]he appeal of Marguerite's ideas to bookish young women who knew that they were being raised as bluestocking marriage bait was ready made" (p. 351). Details of the poem's production and circulation are usually pushed aside by treatments of the poem's content, but this was a work designed to show up *elsewhere*, its Latin an unusual choice for a Protestant text. The *Hecatodistichon* aims to reach outside England and the court of Edward and to match Protector Somerset's bid for international prestige by mapping out the ways dynastic power is entrenched in families.[28] Published in Paris by their tutor Nicolas Denisot—who may have also been a member of Marguerite's court and later a spy for Henri II—the poem, a collection of alternating distichs in praise of Marguerite, was followed a year later by a new edition, the *Tombeau*, which reissues the poem in a commemorative volume. The *Tombeau* also includes tributes to the Seymour sisters themselves, "Maiden Sisters and English Heroines," according to French poets like du Bellay and Ronsard.[29]

Whereas Elizabeth describes the female sinner as biologically, spiritually, and emotionally linked to and defined by her God, the Seymour's poem envisions Marguerite as defying death, nature, and space, as well as all linguistic, imaginative, and intellectual limits: 'Away with physicians; away with the skills of Machaon. She who will not die is in the hands of her doctor" (line 29). Marguerite's powers are immense and even seductive here. Demers rightly emphasizes the epithalamic imagery throughout the Seymours' poem illustrating the rewards and rest promised by a heavenly marriage bed (line 90, line 100), in stark contrast to Elizabeth's repeated references to adultery and maternal neglect. Unlike Elizabeth, the Seymours also emphasize Marguerite's "queenly" status, as Demers notes, too (p. 354). In fact, images of Marguerite's sovereignty and of her "great body" help define what Demers calls Marguerite's "nurturing maternal figure" (see line 2). Saint, lover, and queen, the image of Marguerite allows the Seymour sisters to rectify some of the defects exposed by Elizabeth's translation (and push aside the imagery of holy incest), although oddly they neglect to mention that their king's

---

[27] After Parr's death, Thomas Seymour again attempts a seduction, and then turns his attentions on nine-year-old Jane Grey with the intention of marrying her off to Edward VI. Charged with treason by the Lord Protector and brought to trial, Thomas Seymour is executed in 1549. See James (pp. 307–17) for an extensive discussion of the Seymour family and how conflicts between its members "expanded into the realm of national politics" (p. 312).

[28] See Julie Crawford (2006 B), para 15, for a discussion of the ways that study of the early modern family requires analysis of its political and dynastic goals.

[29] See Demers for additional details about the *Hecatodistichon*'s Paris appearance (pp. 349–57); Prescott also describes its reception (p. 73).

30   *Women's Wealth and Women's Writing in Early Modern England*

sister was the French queen's first translator.[30] The focus remains on Marguerite, but what elevates her is what separates her, and Marguerite transcends rather than sanctifies the family Elizabeth had carefully tried in her translation to recover and rebuild. As Jane Seymour says, "Whatever was in me of spirit served Christ; and on account of this, I am a queen–more than when I was only alive" (line 66).

***

That these young authors thought so deeply about their position as daughters has many early modern origins—some literary, some social, some even biological. Maureen Quilligan (2005) points to one of the biological motives in noting the peculiarly non-exogamous status of Henry's two daughters, given the incest narratives surrounding accounts of their legitimacy and royal standing (pp.35–6). The Seymour sisters temporarily fall into this category of unmarriageable daughters as well after their father is imprisoned and then executed, their mother jailed too for a time after charges of insurrection against Edward VI are brought upon them. Perhaps at times of immense political and personal crisis, these young women were reduced to the sorry state of daughters who could not be traded or transformed: Wordsworth's Lucy Gray or Wharton's Charity Royall seem like later incarnations; the *Pearl*-poet's dead daughter an earlier one. Such a peculiar status continues to characterize the Tudor sisters: when Mary Tudor *chose* a husband, she selected someone from her mother's family; similarly, as Quilligan notes, Elizabeth's first reported love affair was with her stepmother's husband.

The troubled tie to mothers remains a concern of state, too. During the lord protector's protracted investigation of his brother's efforts to seduce the princess, Elizabeth had alluded to the same disparities of loyalty, obligation, and affection that I have been describing here, the awkward, sometimes painful mismatch between mothers and daughters, especially aristocratic ones, as well as the discrepancy between mothers and other female caregivers. Of course, Elizabeth had long and hard experience of these differences by the age of 16, with a handful of stepmothers and governesses. It is at this point that she writes, in a 1549 letter to the lord protector, to defend her governess Kat Ashley from the same charges of treason that Thomas Seymour had faced:

> First, because that she hath been with me a long time and many years, and has taken great labor and pain of bringing of me up in learning and honesty. And therefore I ought of very duty speak for her, for Saint Gregory sayeth that we are more bound to them that bringeth us up well than to our parents, for our parents do that which is natural for them—that is, bringeth us into this world—but our bringers-up are a cause to make us live well in it. (*Collected Works*, p. 34)

---

[30]   Prescott comments on the Seymour sisters' failure to mention or include Elizabeth's translation of Marguerite, suggesting it "[recalls] the arrogance that had led Somerset's wife to quarrel with Catherine Parr and that would help bring Somerset himself, despite his real virtues, to a second and fatal fall later that year" (p. 76).

It seems strange to have the worlds of children and parents rejected for being natural or sinful, but the literary exercises and needlework projects of early modern girls acknowledge the same difficulties Elizabeth's letter subtly hints at, that a daughter might be bound most to the *other* women who have labored to help her trade a long-forgotten Eden for a world they know and have made together.

Elizabeth's *Miroir or Glasse* served as a receptacle for memory, ambition, and dread. Yet the translation was also a gift, a piece of woman's work that would, in just a few years, be increasingly replaced by the production of commodities for sale, like the miscellany of poems Isabella Whitney publishes in 1573, citing not only her lack of employment but the absence of kin ties as motives for writing. Even the works of Princess Elizabeth and the Seymour sisters hint at this reinvention of maternal space as increasingly privatized and made secret, weakened systematically from within and without. Both Elizabeth and the Seymour sisters also meditate on the emptiness of Marguerite de Navarre's maternal legacy. To be sure, mother's legacies can be ambivalent, even impoverishing, with instructions to adhere to patriarchal rules appearing alongside lessons on self-effacement. "The riddle of daughterhood," as Sandra Gilbert nicely puts it, is an "empty pack," because the mother frequently leaves her child neither her example nor her power but, instead, the incontrovertible fact that the female child that "is [not] and cannot be [the patriarch's] inheritor" (pp. 256–8). For the Seymours, Marguerite's remoteness is finally the source and proof of Marguerite's divine power and of the heavenly reward due her. For Elizabeth, in contrast, Marguerite's remote power becomes a source of her own. In Marguerite's words, moreover, the princess finds both a model and a birthright, a way to encode both indebtedness and renewal.[31] "I feel well that the root of it is in me," Elizabeth notes here—in a vision that would also mark a long reign of peace and remarkable self-sufficiency for sovereign and nation alike—"and outwardly I see no other effect but all is either branch, leaf, or else fruit that she bringeth forth all about me" (Shell, p. 114).

---

[31]   Cf. Quilligan (2005), who maintains that Elizabeth "incorporates into herself all the problematic family relationships of her own life—mother, stepmother, father, brother, sister—and makes them all into the family of the nation she rules alone" (p. 73).

Chapter 2
Borrowed Robes

We are, none of us, "either" mothers or daughters; to our amazement, confusion, and greater complexity, we are both.[1]

The rules surrounding the nature and transmission of women's property in early modern England were remarkably unclear, and mothers were often able, as a consequence, to pass along their wealth with real care, deliberation, and invisibility. Of course, we need to take tremendous pains to define this wealth—be it in terms of personal possessions, familial property including land and jewels, or goods and favors shared by the living. Such a calculus of gifts and debts and resources also reveals something about the economics of gender, that is, the ways that women's (or men's) status and influence might be measured in terms of things that are owned, produced, consumed, or shared with others. But my primary concern in this chapter is more basic. By studying the circulation of women's wealth, I want to recover what it meant to mother in early modern England, because—aside from the often considerable physical demands mothering placed upon many women's energies—mothering also had a significant economic component that women of all classes somehow recognized and aimed to supply, in the form of linens and cloth, jewels and religious objects, medicines, prayers, and advice.

The first part of this chapter explores how many links between mothers and children were, therefore, conceived through material goods. I take, as a particularly striking example, Elizabeth I's use of her sister Mary's coronation robes, and explain Elizabeth's choice of clothing as a way of simultaneously representing, interpreting, and disposing of Mary's legacy. Such recycling of royal garments was actually commonplace in the project of establishing what Joanna Woodall calls a "visual genealogy" (p. 208); but these robes had special significance for the childless and Catholic Mary, such that sharing them with a sister or daughter would have been unlikely, perhaps impossible: Elizabeth would have to borrow or steal them, instead. That the ties between them were tangled, even broken, is a common theme in the adult Elizabeth's letters to Mary, as when the princess admonishes her queen to "remember your last promise and my last demand" (*Collected Works*, p. 41). Promises and demands made between early modern women could assume a variety of shapes, however, and the second part of this chapter considers other ways that women's property circulated in early modern England, in terms of the rules and conventions mother's advice books seek to uncover or establish. I argue

---

[1] Rich, Adrienne. *Of Woman Born: Motherhood as Experience and Institution* (1976). NY: Norton, 1986, p. 253.

here, though, that even these relatively uncomplicated exchanges—at least, ones less conflicted than those between Elizabeth and Mary Tudor—challenge us to look at early modern women's power anew, in terms of the influence they wielded over or objects they might transmit to each other.

***

There were two false pregnancies in the course of Mary Tudor's five-year reign, and one illegitimate heir, Mary's bastard sister, Elizabeth. The devoutly Catholic Mary reluctantly and only obliquely acknowledged her heretical half-sister as her successor in a codicil to her will[2]; and for a brief time after the 1554 Wyatt rebellion, Elizabeth had even been placed under house arrest as a threat-in-waiting. But in earlier years Mary had also acted as a mother to a sister seventeen years her junior and this mothering continued when Mary ascended the throne, for the Queen planned Elizabeth's engagement, provided her with jewels, and insisted upon Elizabeth's observance of Catholic ceremonies. The relationship was always marked by an affection and indebtedness that link mothers and daughters more powerfully than sisters or sovereigns and their subjects.[3]

The relationship between all three Tudor siblings is a fascinating but murky one: Mary and Elizabeth were both rendered illegitimate by their father in an act of state, but Mary was also godmother to her brother Edward (see Levin). As I explored in Chapter 1, the princess Elizabeth had been especially close to her always affectionate stepmother Katherine Parr (only four years older than Mary), but Parr dies after giving birth in 1548 when Elizabeth is fifteen years old. Elizabeth's relationship with Mary was more longstanding as well as ultimately more demanding. If the two sisters saw little of each other during Edward's short reign, with Mary's accession, their relationship grew more important and more tense. Ann Rosalind Jones and Peter Stallybrass tell us that "fashion" acquired a new meaning in the sixteenth century, now suggesting "counterfeiting" or "perversion" (p. 1), and Elizabeth's fashioning of herself as the queen's sister drew on many disguises to cloak her ambitions and religious leanings. Her letters, like the one I quote from above, frequently reflect such maneuvers. If at one point Elizabeth commiserates with her sister about menstrual pains, at another point such intimacies have been pushed aside by political misunderstanding, and Elizabeth demands a private audience with Mary so as to counteract "the evil persuasions [that] persuade . . . one sister against the other" (*Collected Works*, pp. 37, 42).

Some of these "evil persuasions" were felt more widely than others. Mary's impending motherhood was always more or less an issue during her short reign, with "Midwives, Rockers, Nurses, . . . the Cradle and all, . . . prepared and in a readiness" for its duration, as one pamphlet entitled *Idem iterum, or, The history of Q. Mary's big-belly* suggests, elsewhere registering the queen's discomfiture

---

[2] For details about the succession and about the sisters' relationship more generally, see Starkey, and Loades (esp. pp. 283–90).

[3] Other critics have, usually indirectly, pointed to this reading of the sisters' relationship. See Arnold (1988, p. 4), Somerset (1991, pp. 32–40), and Starkey (pp. 24–5, 120–28).

in the gross terms of "Spanish Hearts being carried in English Bodies" and the Prophet Jonas "safely deliver[ed]" out of the Whale's Belly (rpt. Foxe, 1688). Mary's mothering burdened Elizabeth, too, implicating her in a relationship that would continue beyond the grave. As Mary was dying, Carrolly Erickson reports, the queen sent a servant to Hatfield to give Mary's jewels to Elizabeth in return for the promise of three things: "[T]hat she would uphold the Catholic faith, take care of Mary's servants, and pay [Mary's] debts" (Erickson, 1978, p. 481).

When Elizabeth is crowned a few months after Mary's death in November 1558, she wears the very same robes Mary had worn for her own coronation. This unusual sartorial decision—especially given their troubled tie (and Elizabeth's later reputation as a clotheshorse[4])—is a way for Elizabeth both to reify and obliterate her connection to Mary Tudor, revealing herself as both Mary's heir and her foil. Even royal women made recourse to traditional female practices of gift-giving in their borrowings and letters, as well as in their self-display. Women of all classes similarly traded on the meanings of mothering, and such practices are reflected in—and may have shaped—a tradition of women's writing in early modern England. And, as I explore at the close of this chapter, many of these writings are preoccupied with both the importance and fungibility of maternal ties.

Of course, Queen Elizabeth's later extravagance was matched by an equally well-known penuriousness, and Mary's regalia was state treasure, to be disposed of by the crown. Yet Elizabeth's choice of clothing on such a formative day has a variety of meanings and supports a variety of values, some of them official, some more personal, all of them helping us to understand what women's wealth consisted of, and to whom it most properly belonged. At the outset, I would suggest that Elizabeth's decision has something to do with controlling reproduction: the reproduction of cloth, most obviously, but through this activity the reproduction of power, relations, and influence (see Crawford, 1990): it, therefore, reworks once more the ambiguous relationship between mothers and children in early modern England. Scholars like Betty S. Travitsky (2001) maintain that both Renaissance humanists and Protestant reformers accorded early modern mothers more intellectual and spiritual influence over their children than medieval mothers could claim (p. iv), yet the real nature of this power—who really possesses it, how it is wielded, what it shapes—is less clear, as the many manuals and treatises written by English women during this time indicate, again and again. Lady Macbeth's evocation of the nursing child whose brains she would dash out is an example of the cruel license early modern mothers could take or deep affections they might easily abandon; yet Elizabeth's use of her sister's coronation robes implies that children might reinterpret or relinquish these relations themselves, given the chance. If Mary's robes illustrate the maternal influence she possessed and how it might continue after Mary's death, on the one hand, they also tell us

---

[4] See Arnold (1988, p. 98).

Women's Wealth and Women's Writing in Early Modern England

how Tudor genealogy might be reconstituted by Elizabeth herself in her very first act as monarch, on the other hand, with the help of a court tailor.[5]

***

Painted more than 40 years after the fact, the 1600 "Coronation Portrait" of Queen Elizabeth I shows her wearing the same ermine trimmed robes at her 1559 coronation that Mary had worn five-and-a-half years earlier. Janet Arnold, who has produced an exhaustive inventory of Elizabeth's clothing during the years of her long reign, briefly comments on this borrowing and the feelings it symbolizes, suggesting that "[t]he robes of 'clothe of gold and silver tissue' which [Elizabeth] had watched her sister wear in 1553, must have seemed like a triumphant and tangible symbol of safety and freedom" (Arnold, 1978, p. 728). Their symbolism is still more ambitious, however: identical dress would seem to untangle the complicated relationship between the sisters by making Mary's ambiguous legacy appear ready-made for Elizabeth, something that she might appropriately recycle— or at least easily remake. Mary Tudor's will was similarly equivocal, revealing a twinned discomfort with and confidence in her successor's natural abilities: "[M]y said heyre and Successour," Mary writes, "will supplye the Imperfection of my said will and testament therein, & accomplishe and fynishe the same accordynge to my true mynde and intente" (Loades, p. 382). The suggestion is that Elizabeth would not only adhere to but realize Mary's best designs for the English church and England's people, even for herself. And what better way to appropriate Mary's own iconography than to wear it on one's back?[6]

Elizabeth had many mothers to "think back through," as Virginia Woolf describes the work of daughters (p. 76), and we might view Elizabeth's long career as somehow organized by this rethinking of her history. Still, why risk the specter of Mary's ghost at the coronation festivities, designed by reformers, according to contemporary accounts, to exorcise this Catholic figure? Elizabeth's royal apparel conjures up other magical dresses and other investiture ceremonies, too, where the putting on of clothes becomes a sovereign act (see Jones and Stallybrass, p. 2). Whether early modern spectators were reminded of the transformed Cinderella (stories of whom were being codified in print at the time)—or even of the beloved Creusa and spurned Medea (whose stories are reflected in contemporary maternal legacies)—the effect of the dress is almost the same—that of a fairy tale gone awry, or unsettling bad dream.[7] There are other drawbacks to imperial hoarding,

---

[5] Arnold (1988) tells us the tailor's name was Walter Fyshe. Additional details about the coronation dress are provided in Arnold (1978, esp. pp. 727–30). For an excellent discussion of Queen Mary I's wardrobe, see Carter.

[6] See Frye (1993) for an examination of Elizabeth's use of Mary's iconography (pp. 43–4).

[7] In the first version of "Cindirella or, the Little Glass Slipper" recorded in English, the degraded princess is given a "dress of cloth of gold and silver, all beset with jewels." This version, translated by Robert Samber in his *Histories, or Tales of Past Times*, by M. Perrault (London, 1729), is reprinted by Iona and Peter Opie (see p. 125). The earliest

Fig. 2.1 The "Coronation Portrait" of Elizabeth I (1600) by an unknown artist. Painted near the end of the sixty-seven-year-old queen's reign, Elizabeth is wearing the borrowed robes of her sister.

as Shakespeare often notes, the widespread practice sometimes regarded as an example of bad taste: "Thrift, thrift, Horatio," the sardonic Hamlet tells his friend, explaining why the "funeral baked meats" served after his father's burial "[d]id coldly furnish forth" the marriage tables of his mother and uncle (1.2). Shakespeare's reading of royal economy is rendered with less irony in Macbeth, where the king's men complain that Macbeth's stolen title hangs loosely about him, "like a giant's robe / Upon a dwarfish thief" (5.2).

Women's clothing belongs to a more complicated category, however, since their property was typically under a husband or father's supervision. Elizabeth rather than Philip took possession of Mary's robes after her death because this was state property; to Mary's husband were returned many of the jewels he had given his wife during their marriage, because they belonged to the Spanish crown.[8] There were, indeed, an assortment of loopholes in the laws and practices governing women's goods, and recent studies have not only helped us trace where women's possessions might go, but also how extensive and significant were women's goods at the time, their distribution not only informing coronation ceremonies but the very structure of society (see Erickson, 1993, p. 4; and Korda, 2002, pp. 1–7). Women's material objects substantiate families, underpin affections, and organize households; and the fact that their things are so easily lost or traded or resewn makes them more rather than less valuable, easier to circulate.

***

Queens and kings often wore the clothing and jewels of predecessors for reasons of economy and tradition. Janet Arnold also points out that clothes were frequently left as bequests in wills because of the value of the material: many of Elizabeth's gowns, Arnold reports, were "trauncelated" into furnishings after her death or given to players, the pearls and spangles sold, other items given to her ladies-in-waiting.[9] But the translation of royal regalia could have the public effect of denuding Elizabeth's predecessor, playing up her memory by transforming

---

published version of the tale appears in Italy in 1634, although it likely circulated much earlier in oral form: part of the 1540 *Complaynt of Scotland* includes the tale of Rashin Coatie, in which a coat of rushes arouses the jealousy of a lovely girl's stepmother. Clothes are at the center of both of these stories, although in the Grimm's version, clothing plays a lesser part—a synecdoche of a synecdoche—when the heroine is identified by a missing slipper. Details of the Scottish story are provided by Opie and Opie, pp. 117–18. For the connection to Creusa, I am indebted to Feroli, who makes a persuasive case for Elizabeth Jocelin's anxiety about such a maternal image in her 1624 text (p. 95, see also pp. 97–9). Johnson explores how (and why) such monstrous images of mothers are shaped.

[8] Additional details about Philip's gifts of jewelry to Mary are supplied by Woodall (p. 223 n75).

[9] See Carter (p.17); Arnold (1988, pp. xiv, 98, 175). Elsewhere Arnold (1980) comments: "The use of an earlier material is not unusual. There are hundreds of references to the remodeling of gowns for Queen Elizabeth's personal use, as well as for her ladies-in-waiting, sometimes over ten years after they were first made." Arnold adds: "Expensive materials were used over and over again, as long as they were in good condition" (p. 72 n57).

Mary into a ghost. In adopting the livery of her older sister and thereby advertising her established position in Mary's royal household, Elizabeth at the same time buries her sister's royal claims: if clothes make the queen, Mary has been royally divested.[10] There were, though, many reasons for Elizabeth to promote aggressively Mary's image at the same time. Like Mary, Elizabeth assumed the throne as an unmarried queen regnant, not as a queen consort, and what little precedent existed for this unusual and uncomfortable state of affairs in England (aside from the disastrous reign of Matilda in the twelfth century) had to be followed to the letter: wearing something second-hand in this case made tremendous political sense.

Yet Mary had cleared Elizabeth's royal path in many other ways, and in wearing the same dress, Elizabeth was also emulating a Mary herself constrained by precedent, deliberately dressed down for her own coronation, because the "clothe of gold and silver tissue" was actually that of a queen consort rather than that of a queen regnant. Judith M. Richards (2005) maintains, indeed, that "it is vital to understand just how much Elizabeth owed to Mary . . . [who was] older at her succession, better prepared for rule, and always widely recognized as a virtuous woman." Actually, Richards maintains, Mary was "a much more acceptable candidate by law, descent and reputation" than was her sister (p. 12). Part of Mary's acceptability is also explained by some of the steps she took on her coronation day, for the unmarried queen presented herself as a "less than fully royal monarch," with the loose hair of a bride, an open rather than closed crown, and a dress of white cloth of gold, not the purple robes of a king.[11] Such a circumscribed image of sovereignty gives her heir room to maneuver; but perhaps Elizabeth borrows the royal garment of a queenly virgin exactly because this was something the childless Mary could not bequeath a daughter. Elizabeth allows Mary a legacy, in other words, while underscoring its emptiness.

There was enormous religious motivation behind Elizabeth's decision as well. Protestant reformers in England strategically made use of Catholic relics, including priestly vestments and altar cloths, to unveil or discharge those items'

Jones and Stallybrass explore such borrowing and make reference to Elizabeth's recycling habits as well (p. 26), but do not discuss her use of Mary's robes.

[10] See Jones and Stallybrass on investiture robes (p. 2); household livery (p. 5); and how the medieval concept of the king's "two bodies" might be explained with reference to a queen or king subject to infirmity or death and the royal clothes that would outlast this figure (p. 196).

[11] See also Richards 1997 (pp. 897, 900–901). Richards explains that "it was during Mary's reign that accommodations consequent upon the occupation of the traditionally male monarchy by the first female occupant were devised. Those strategies subsequently defined central symbolic forms of Elizabeth's reign and shaped their readings" (p. 895). Under different circumstances, however, Mary would insist upon her position as queen regnant. As Richards (2003) comments, "[M]ost remarkable was the path [Mary] followed in her marriage to a foreign prince while preserving her legal autonomy" (p. 28). Margaret Scott of the Courtauld Institute made a similar point about the precedent of Mary as queen regnant in a personal communication.

ritual magic, turning them into furnishings for Protestant homes or costumes for professional players (Jones and Stallybrass, p. 192). The Catholic Mary Stuart would allow herself such iconoclastic impulses, too, when she recycled altar cloths confiscated from Aberdeen Chapel into a bedspread for her lover's apartments (Swain, 1973, p. 51). Stuart's scandalous artistry provides the subject of the next chapter; for now, I want simply to suggest that what seems like a rough handling of weighty theological matter actually has a rationale. Protestants who rejected the Catholic doctrine of transubstantiation, whereby the eucharistic bread and wine were literally transformed into Christ's body and blood, nonetheless exploited the magic and simply reversed the charm when they repackaged Catholic relics rather than disposing of them altogether.[12] We need to keep in mind, too, that the London of 1559 was still more Catholic than Protestant, and Elizabeth's religious impulses ran along several lines, suppressing as many religious questions as possible (Frye, 1993, p. 45): William P. Haugaard tells us, for instance, that the consecrated host was not elevated at the coronation mass, even though Elizabeth was crowned according to the rites of a Latin liturgy (p. 170). Similarly, instead of tearing up Mary's Catholic costume for a queen, Elizabeth had a new bodice and pair of sleeves made for the kirtle.[13] What better way to retain the appearance of things, while neatly and quietly altering the substance underneath?

***

More than 50 years later, Mary Stuart's niece Arbella will sell off the embroidered panels Mary had worked on in captivity in order to finance her own escape from one of James's jails (see Steen, *Letters*, p. 160). That women's belongings were meager and that their distribution frequently marked the rupture rather than the cementing of ties between them is explicitly taken up in Isabella Whitney's "Wyll and Testament," a poem that appears in an anthology entitled *A Sweet Nosgay* published in 1573. In fact, the poem's twinned subjects are alienation and authority, for Whitney distributes to her readers things she can neither own nor share, but more simply those things she "shal leave behinde" (line 22). The poem is strangely reminiscent of the children's game of hot potato, where the goal is to get rid of something in order to find oneself bereft: indeed, Whitney closes the poem by exorcising consumption, telling her readers: "[M]ay your wants exile" (line 276). With a similar emphasis on the traps of consumption, Natasha Korda (2002) describes the responsibilities of women as housewives in the early modern period, their moral duty and social standing increasingly centered on the preservation of "houshold stuff," more and more of it consumer goods acquired through their husbands' efforts, not their own. Many of Shakespeare's

---

[12] Greenblatt argues that the Eucharistic wafer was to the Renaissance imagination the "sublime object of ideology," "an entirely chimerical entity, impossible to grasp except by tracking its traumatic effects" (p. 338). Additional details on the Protestant destruction—or reconstruction—of Catholic symbols and objects are offered by Duffy, and Mazzola (1998).

[13] Arnold (1988) analyzes the methods and results of this "translation" in rich detail (pp. 52–7).

Borrowed Robes 41

plays, Korda notes, explore the complicated new economic rules that encouraged acquisition but faulted spending: new wives Kate and Desdemona are criticized by their husbands for being irresponsible consumers (careless with caps and handkerchiefs, for instance) rather than capable managers of households, much less as producers of important goods.[14]

***

Shakespeare rarely represents the ties between mothers and daughters in his plays; of the few instances, we have *The Winter's Tale*, where the absent Hermione is recovered as a piece of "houshold stuff" herself after her daughter Perdita matures, a picture of consumption (one her husband Leontes validates as "lawful as eating") that makes a mother literally disappear into the home. Hermione's magic is moral, her morality mostly aesthetic, and her powerlessness not unlike that of other early modern mothers, Mary Tudor among them, with confusions surrounding their possessions, authority, and ability to transfer either one.[15] These confusions allow Elizabeth to use her sister's robes so readily, transforming—or "counterfeiting"—state property into more private paraphernalia. We know that, with the exception of such paraphernalia, women's property belonged to their husbands, and so advice books written by mothers often begin with an apology for their presumption of male duties or authority in drafting such documents (Wall, 1991, pp. 44–5). Such advice books, five of which appear in rapid succession after Elizabeth's death, outline a specifically female world of caring, knowledge, and transmission. Many of them are self-deprecating, like the pregnant Elizabeth Jocelin's 1622 tract, her "little legacy," as she calls it, consisting of "a few weake instructions cominge from a dead mother" (See Brown, 1999, pp. 106, 111). Elizabeth Grymeston's epistle to her son similarly describes her imaginative limitations as bodily ones, even as she seeks to disown them: "And the spiders webbe is neither the better because wouen out of his own brest, nor the bees hony the woorse for that gathered out of many flowers: neither could I euer brooke to set down that haltingly in my broken stile, which I found better expressed by a grauer author." Yet these advice books also often articulate another way of calculating and sharing wealth: Dorothy Leigh, in *The Mothers Blessing* (1616), likens unheard advice to "many mens garments motheate in their chests, while their Christian bretheren quake with cold in the street for want of couering."[16] Marked thus both by power and decay, Mary's dress shares with these writings the riddle of maternal influence, presenting claims about women's property and authority while detaching them from the mother.

***

In *A Room of One's Own*, Virginia Woolf poses the same riddle in exploring the faulty distribution of women's property: "What had our mothers been doing then," this impoverished child rudely wonders, "that they had no wealth to leave us?" (p. 21).

---

[14] See Korda (2002) for details about women's household stuff.

[15] Following Korda (2002), we might ask whether increasing control over a relatively isolated household gave women more or less influence over each other (p. 12).

[16] Grymeston's tract is reprinted in Travitsky (2001, p. 4).

But Woolf's focus on economics ironically omits the rich material world that wives and mothers inhabit and routinely recreate. Studying cloth bestowal and exchange in twentieth-century Oceania and the Trobriand Islands, recent anthropologists supply us with a radically different picture of women's wealth. Many of their accounts focus on the ways that cloth is especially crucial to its accrual and exchange. In Oceania, for example, cloth mats woven by women are prized both for their sheer value and for their ability to link kin groups and obligations; indeed, as Jane Schneider and Annette B. Weiner argue, such items are so imbued with sacred and ancestral referents that they have "socially protective powers" (p. 13). Studying related practices in Madagascar, where clothing is demanded by the dead as part of a complicated and protracted series of burial rituals, Gillian Feeley-Harnik suggests that clothing is a "product of reciprocity" (p. 78), a precious material that articulates otherwise unspoken relationships. Of course, we have to be careful in drawing connections between contemporary small-scale societies and the social world of early modern England, but there are some useful similarities. Defining ancestors, maintaining lineages and identifying progeny, sumptuary codes regulating cloth distribution and display operate in small-scale societies much as they did in early modern England, where mourning robes were distributed by kin of the deceased at funerals as a way to "channel death into regeneration and political gain" (cf. Schneider and Weiner, p. 11). What anthropological accounts also tell us is that if, by definition, clothing is practical, superficial, and decorative, it is also always a rich and valuable tool precisely because of its power to "fashion from within" (Jones and Stallybrass, p. 2) and to recreate the wearer as part of its symbolism.

The connections between women and cloth are especially important in both worlds as well. In her study of South Pacific societies, Weiner examines how women's weaving holds kin groups together, transmitting material wealth and influence in ways that Woolf's powerful account of a female tradition cannot register. After a death, Trobriand women bleach, dry, and fashion skirts from banana leaf fibers and distribute these bundles on behalf of the dead so as to ensure the continued stability of the deceased's family. Weiner views this project as the "transformation of women's reproductive capacity into an object" (p. 61). Part of this wealth, however, continues to belong to the giver. Describing mats woven by Samoan women, Weiner points out that such objects can circulate and yet still be "inalienable," identified as a treasure that significantly reinforces the giver's position.[17] In Weiner's account, cloth is protective, binding, and concealing. Hoarding or selling cloth—as I explore more fully in Chapter 5—is a terrible crime against this women's world of circulating goods and ongoing relationships, refusals to reproduce the logic that weaves kin, interests, and debts.

For similar reasons, Lear tells his daughter Regan to "reason not the need" for his own fastidious requirements for sumptuous living (2.4). The garments of power in Shakespeare's plays may simply be the clothes on a king's back, but their obviousness

---

[17] Weiner (pp. 35, 46), passim. Quilligan (2000) makes reference to the work of Weiner in describing Princess Elizabeth Tudor's gift to her stepmother, which Quilligan says "looks oddly like the trade in women's heirloom items that Annette Weiner finds generic to female communities" (pp. 220–21).

makes them no less necessary, and no less gorgeous. In *King Lear*, as Margreta de Grazia writes, "Clothes rank as the play's representative superfluous thing," but Lear, nonetheless, "shakes the superflux by disrobing" (p. 23). Yet there are still other interests—more communal than Lear's private need to be recognized—created and protected by female cloth wealth that can be hoarded or banked, torn, shared, or left to rot. "[S]uch treasure," Schneider and Weiner argue, "facilitates claims to the past—its names, legends, and events—that justify the transactions and extend the power of living actors" (p. 6). A matriarchal world of obligation and likeness is also created in the process, assuming shape by describing ties to female relatives or by incurring debts to them (see Feeley-Harnik, pp. 73–4). Elizabeth capitalizes on this process of producing mothers and daughters at her coronation, for her appropriation of a dead sister's dress at once symbolizes Mary's ancestry as well as Mary's inability to reproduce such a relation.

***

The existence of a female literary tradition in early modern England was likewise premised, Wendy Wall (1991) argues, on the language of legacy. This carefully crafted network of maternal ties helped female authors emerge and then, Wall suggests, explain themselves away, their wills and advice books and poetry "a strangely performative and self-constituting gesture dependent upon the erasure of the subject."[18] If female authorship was legitimated through the process of making real women disappear, so was motherhood itself, not only reconstructed as a literary, political, and social rather than biological fact, but also codified, amplified, or sometimes reorganized, especially in mother's advice books. Such works are various and extensive, treating pregnancy, prayer, courtship, child-rearing, marriage, and household management. Reading them gives us a better idea of the manifold circumstances under which mothering was permitted in early modern England.

For one thing, many of the immensely popular advice books written by women in the sixteenth and seventeenth centuries in England are premised on the death of the author.[19] Upon learning of her pregnancy, for example, Elizabeth Jocelin (1596–1622) embarks on *The Mothers Legacie, to her unborne Childe* (1624) only after she buys her winding sheet.[20] (Elsewhere, she undercuts her work not only because it derives from her, but because it is addressed to a child.) The always looming fear

---

[18]   Wall (1991, pp. 36, 38). Ashelford adds another wrinkle to Elizabeth's fashion decision, suggesting how early-modern women in England might literally be lost in their clothes. The symmetry characteristic of clothes when Elizabeth ascended the throne—"the triangular shape of the skirt in perfect balance with the inverted triangular shape" of the bodice and extended hanging sleeves—ultimately would give way, by the end of her reign, to a "bizarre silhouette created by extensive stiffening and padding, and so encrusted with decoration that the natural female form entirely disappeared" (p. 11).

[19]   Feroli claims that "the act of writing itself necessarily compels women to realize the terms of their negation," and she therefore reads Jocelin's text as "an autobiography of a lost self" (p. 91). For an overview of maternal advice books, see Beilin (pp. 257–85).

[20]   See Travitsky (2001, pp. xii); (1980, pp. 33–4).

that she might die in childbirth allowed a woman to write in a patriarchal culture that otherwise encouraged female silence (Travitsky, 2001, p. ix). Adhering to this harsh convention, what mothers often give their children in these works is permission—and sometimes, overt and precise instructions—to ignore them. If mothers' advice books therefore ensure a maternal legacy otherwise unavailable, the weakened authority of mothers is thus contradictory at best and always immaterial, premised, as Teresa Feroli puts it, upon the "dissolution of the female body" (p. 91) or upon the insistent renunciations of a mother's language. These books offer other telling examples of an embattled or indebted authority. Elizabeth Grymeston's reference to her "broken stile" in her 1604 tract is one way of understanding maternal borrowings, where women's writings often "inscribe" memory and conflict by including excerpts from other texts. Jones and Stallybrass point to similar uncertainties introduced by recycled cloths. "Whose name is materialized in cloth?" they ask: "The name of the spinner, the weaver, the tailor, the giver of livery, the previous wearer, the present wearer?" (p. 32).

Similar questions surrounding mother's legacies make the 1622 appearance of *The Countesse of Lincolnes Nurserie* (published 1628) all the more surprising. Written by Elizabeth Clinton (1574–1630), the *Nurserie* is directed specifically at new mothers (not at Clinton's children) and focuses on the importance of breast-feeding, a practice that had been nearly eclipsed for elite women by what publisher Thomas Lodge calls the "unnaturall practise" of wet nursing. Male writers like Erasmus in "The New Mother" (1524) and William Gouge in *Of Domesticall Duties* (1622) had adopted a similar stance (see Wayne, pp. 61–2; Travitsky, 1980, p. 42n10), so more interesting to me than why Clinton takes the position (after failing to nurse any of her own 18 children) is the fact that, unlike other mothers' advice books, Clinton's argument emphasizes the regular, sustained, and physical presence of the mother. In Clinton's eyes, the mother's legacy is contingent upon her survival, not upon her death, her influence solely communicated and guaranteed by her body, not by its products or possessions.

The circulation of women's wealth accomplished via the exchange of banana leaf skirts guarantees that giving away something of value ensures its magical influence without consuming the maker. Clinton's outline of female influence transmitted through breast milk—whereby, Lodge explains to the reader, the "stores" of mothers are drained so as to nourish the strength and continuity of their lines–shares this definition of female wealth by erasing any divisions between what a mother can give her children and what continues to be owned by her. [21] At the same time, mother's milk really issues from God's grace, as the pious Clinton explains in her dedication: "I thinke it an honour vnto you, to doe that which hath proued you to be full of care to please God, and of naturall affection, and to bee

---

[21] Citing Weiner's work, Quilligan (2005) explores aristocratic women's efforts to capitalize on the wealth and prestige of their natal families.

well stored with humility, and patience." [22] Indeed, all of the maternal virtues Clinton enumerates find their source in God's bounty: "[H]e is also All sufficient, [and] therefore infinitely able to blesse his owne ordinance, and to afford vs meanes in our selues" (p. 2). That women's possessions really belong to or emanate from men is reiterated by Grymeston's *Miscelanea. Meditations. Memoratives*, which consists of proverbs, prayers, quotations, and paraphrases from Catholic Church fathers, often in the original Latin or Greek. Like many male authors of the time, Grymeston describes her work as a conduit for wisdom that circulates elsewhere, not something that solely belongs to or originates in her, her writings obvious hand-me-downs in a literary world shaped by the coterie (and, therefore, nearly closed) circulation of literary works rather than their more open (and unregulated) exchange and consumption in the marketplace. [23]

Clinton's vision could not be more different, however, since breast-feeding makes possible the transfer of specifically maternal wealth. The uninterrupted tie and unmediated influence made possible via breast-feeding allow the mother— and only her—to become a crucial part of both the outer and inner world of the child, as a source of support, affection, nourishment, and discipline throughout her child's life. Recalling the precept "which willeth the younger women" "to Beare [children] in the wombe," Clinton explains that this sustenance also means mothers "Beare [children] on their knee, in their armes, and at their breasts" (p. 6). According to Clinton's account, mothering is a ongoing event which utilizes all of a woman's physical and moral powers, conflating "the various parts of the body— knee, arm, breast—in [a] continuing natural process of reproduction." "The new mother," Marilyn Luecke argues, "is not only redeemed by breastfeeding; she is also empowered" (p. 244).Clinton's images of maternal ties involve at once a continuous experience and a remarkably closed one, seemingly impervious to outside influence, without even a wish for any other connection. Articulated through mother's milk, such ties also imagine the early modern home as the premier setting for inalienable goods and inalienable ties, a refuge from the marketplace and a site of worship, an antidote to unchecked consumption, and an Eden without wet-nurses.

***

Despite Clinton's convictions about breast-feeding, however, there also runs throughout her treatise a sad and profound skepticism about the definition or duration of maternal ties because of a deep uncertainty over what early modern women might supply each other. One objection, "found by grieuous experience" is to the "dissembling in nurses" who pretend "sufficiency of milke, when indeed

---

[22] See Luecke's valuable study, which suggests how Clinton not only naturalizes the mother's role but also elevates it above the father's.

[23] I am grateful to John Archer for the distinction between an open and closed system of exchange; Donawerth draws a similar contrast in her analysis of early modern women's gift exchanges (p. 5). For additional details on Grymeston, see Martin (p. 101), and Travitsky (1996, p. 236).

they had too much scarcitie" (p. 18). Even when so closely associated with a woman's body, female wealth is not only unusually subject to decay—as Weiner and Feeley-Harnik also contend—but to counterfeiting and artifice, too. [24] Also striking is the strange genealogy Clinton supplies of nursing mothers depicted in the Bible: citing the motherless fallen Eve, the long barren Sarah, and the Virgin Mary, Clinton summons up a world without daughters, a set of precedents without influence. The bonds between mothers and children can be endangered in other ways, particularly, Clinton notes, by money: she warns upper-class mothers not to trust "other women, whom wages hyres to doe it, better than your selves, whom God, and nature ties to doe it" (pp. 17–18). Indeed, cosmic "disorder" ensues from the practice of wetnursing, when the hired nurse is separated from her own offspring in order to care for the children of wealthy mothers. "Be not so unnatural to thrust away your own children," Clinton now admonishes these upper-class mothers: "Be not so hardy as to venture a tender baby to a less tender heart. Be not accessory to that disorder of causing a poorer woman to banish her owne infant for the entertaining of a richer woman's child, as it were, bidding her unloue her owne to love yours" (p. 19). Elsewhere, the *Nurserie* envisions the practice of wetnursing in terms of a suffering explicitly unrelieved by substitution or exchange, a nightmarish fairy tale replete with "lukewarm" mothers and "orphans" (*Nurserie*, p. 4), "queens," "princesses," "Dragons," and "Ostriches" (pp. 19, 4, 8). This is a setting where few mothers' love is bestowed fully or correctly, and where sustenance is replaced—as it is in the London that Whitney parcels out in her *Wyll*—by crime (lines 157–60) and infection (line 151) (see also Luecke, p. 242).

The failure to breastfeed thus accounts for a host of political, cosmological, and economic problems; following Clinton's guidelines creates, in contrast, what Luce Irigaray has called an "economy of abundance" that endlessly renews both subjects and objects and rewrites consumption as slaking desire. [25] With this grand aim in mind, Clinton gives us a definition of mothering that centers on its powers and privileges, suggesting that "to be a noursing mother, is a Queens honour" (p. 17). Obviously Clinton's summons was not powerful enough to counter the demands or satisfactions created by early modern commodity culture, however, where increasingly material things might shape both consumers and the way consumers related to each other. Late-sixteenth century samplers (like the one reproduced in Chapter 1) similarly attest to the fragile, implicit state of links between many early modern women and to the collective anonymity now fostered between mothers and daughters in an increasingly isolated domestic sphere. One pattern book of the period explains: "So Maids may (from their Mistresse, or their

---

[24] In extraordinary detail, Paster explores some of these early-modern fears about bodies and fluids.

[25] Irigaray's phrase is quoted by Donawerth (p. 18). Such a community of women is typified, at least temporarily, by the one that takes shape during the period of childbirth and lying-in, when mothers and mothers-in-law, sisters, aunts, and neighbors surround and support the new mother and child. See Crawford's 1990 essay.

Borrowed Robes 47

Mother)/ Learne to leave one worke, and to learn another," [26] suggesting how maternal ties have at once become widespread and tenuous, easily replaced and occasionally even abandoned.

***

What kind of literary tradition might take shape from the daughters who chose to write in the early modern period? As I explore more fully in Chapter 5, Isabella Whitney offers a nice figure for their abilities and obstacles when she describes her "wylling minde" in the "Wyll and Testament" (lines 21–4), the implication being that we learn about women's ideas by knowing what they have taught themselves to relinquish. Elizabeth's use of Mary's robes should be understood in this light, too, as a way of perceiving what she would claim and make a mother forego, and more broadly in terms of an early modern ambivalence about maternal ties, their extent and meaning and power, the doubts whether they even exist or can continue. Elizabeth spent much of her youth trying to respond to these doubts and puzzle out her relation to her stepmothers and half-sister. At one point, the princess Elizabeth signs a 1554 letter to Mary, by then her queen, as "Your highness' most faithful subject that hath been from the beginning and will be to my end" (*Collected Works*, p. 42). Later, Elizabeth will refashion such loyalty—or self-abasement—and convert Mary into her mother by appropriating her sister's costume as queen, acquiescence to tradition or to the status quo now a most powerful tool of self-assertion (see Frye, 1993, pp. 24–30). Family feeling inspires official repudiation, as we see in Elizabeth's first speech before Parliament on February 10, 1559, where she refuses to group Mary with enemies of the crown, explaining, "I will not now burden her therewith, because I will not charge the dead" (*Collected Works*, p. 57). Courtesy and abjection are yoked together here to make history and relocate maternal feeling to the past.

Mothers, even dead ones, were powerful figures in the early modern period precisely because their influence was indirect, the ultimate source of their power unclear. To be sure, in Elizabeth Clinton's imagination, breast-feeding provides at once a profoundly regenerative physical, theological, emotional, and social connection, knitting together mothers and children, women with women, and believers to their God. It also envisions maternal love as infinite and rich, with a power to rival that of Shakespeare's childless Cleopatra (also decked, Enobarbus tells us, in "cloth of gold"), who "makes hungry / Where most she satisfies" [27] (2.2).

---

[26] Quoted in Frye (1999), who describes pattern books that themselves circulated as valuable commodities, treasured forms of female wealth (p. 176).

[27] Cf. Paster's description of Cleopatra suckling an asp: "Its suckling keeps the maternal body from paternal appropriation; it participates in a conspiracy that uses the nursing bond to defeat and embarrass the father, to deny his disciplinary goals for the maternal body" (pp. 239–40). Perhaps Paster's image of the nursing Cleopatra contrasts so sharply with my picture of the depriving mother because Paster never describes breast milk as a kind of female property or wealth passed down to descendants: like blood, breast milk leaks or flows, according to Paster: it is never shared or given.

It is this image of a royal power to abolish memory which Elizabeth summons up when she puts on Mary's old robes, where a mother's love is endlessly renewable, but also something an ungrateful child might override, reconstruct, or merely choose to put away.

Chapter 3
"Manifest Housekeepers"

I am resolved rather to die a queen, than a private woman.[1]

Even the most private of spaces has its own architecture and rationale and what amounts to a "logic of power," some mechanism for determining what this space means, what kinds of expression it permits.[2] The inhabitants of close or closed quarters may spend more time in conflict with each other than in rebellion against their confines. Shakespeare exposes the tension which can both organize and divide private space in *Coriolanus*, where housebound wife and mother Virgilia and Volumnia, "manifest housekeepers" (1.3),[3] sit and sew together, awaiting news of their kinsman, the warrior Coriolanus. Coupled so closely together, the paired images illustrate age-old discord between in-laws,[4] and the spite that orders this particular world is obvious; but Shakespeare also suggests that the early modern household could be a claustrophobic setting for solitude and for pride—a "brewing place of poisons" rather than a "protected place of withdrawal" (see Ziegler, p. 85)—where anxious sublimation ranges unintelligibly alongside fierce and radical revision.

In Mary Stuart's short career, we find the same picture of household strife, uneasy isolation crowded alongside proud retirement. Uncomfortably confined within a series of English houses under lock and key for 19 years, Mary was both a state secret and public enemy, subject to official rumor as well as scarcely detectable maneuverings in her jail in central England. If Mary's prison cell could also be called a rival court with priests, a dozen ladies and gentlemen and their personal servants, laundresses, a doctor, a baker, four stable boys, messengers (or spies), and her chair and cloth of estate (see Lovell, p. 218), it was still a dreary setting for a dowager queen and potential successor to Elizabeth. And if only seemingly invisible to the larger early modern world of which she was such

---

[1] *The Letters of Mary Stuart* 169; hereafter, all references to this edition will be cited as *Letters* and noted parenthetically in the text.

[2] Jones (1990) is quoting Stuart Hall (p. 4).

[3] See Ziegler's description of the type of "normative Woman" that had become an ideal by Shakespeare's time: "[S]he is 'housebound'; she lives vicariously through the news that others bring her and through the historiated tapestries on her walls, she associates primarily with her maid" (p. 80). The solitary Ophelia sewing in her closet is another example of Shakespeare's "normative Woman" but her isolation, as Ziegler comments, makes her vulnerable to Hamlet's suspicions (p. 85).

[4] Orlin (1999) refers to this scene as illustrating a "generational subtext" (p. 193).

a formative part, as Elizabeth's unwelcome guest in England, Mary was often relegated to the margins of much of the intrigue and fervor she inspired.

The first picture of private space that Mary's short career offers is supplied by the sizeable corpus of needlework she left behind, a body of work at once curiously conventional and grandly suited to the designs of a Tudor, Stuart, and Valois queen.[5] Indeed, one scholar concludes that Mary's "increasingly daring circulation" of letters and gifts of needlework during her captivity may have encouraged the development of the Elizabethan secret service.[6] Much of this needlework was produced in concert with her first keeper's wife, Bess of Hardwick, the countess of Shrewsbury. It includes several gifts for Mary's cousin Elizabeth, including night caps, a cushion cover, and a red satin skirt brilliantly embroidered with gold and silver thread that took three months to complete. These gifts were always represented by Mary and Bess as private exchanges between affectionate women, even though Elizabeth never reciprocated (Swain, 1973, pp. 82–4; Klein, 1997, pp. 475–6). There were also gifts for Mary's Catholic friends and allies who repeatedly conspired to free her and depose Elizabeth. Mary's work in addition includes the Oxburgh hangings, four large panels with emblems and ciphers that feature an elaborate complex of personal and political meanings at once subtle and repetitively obvious. I will concentrate upon the Oxburgh hangings in this chapter, although I will also comment on other needlework attributed to Mary's hand.

A second and equally equivocal picture of queenly retirement is supplied by the sequence of love sonnets Mary allegedly wrote to the Earl of Bothwell, her

---

[5]   This work is controversial, both on account of Mary's peculiar history and because of needlework's own complicated meaning for historians and literary scholars. Orlin (1999) notes that John Ford's Annabella "seems less interested in stilling her transgressive thoughts by means of her busy hands than in striking a recognized pose of virtuous industry" (pp.183–4). Parker (1984) makes a similar point, claiming that the needleworker's posture or "position signifies repression and subjugation" (p. iv). More positive readings of women's needlework are offered by Hedges and by Ulrich. For a related discussion of women's art and the history that has ignored it, see Mainardi.

As far as Mary's problematic place in the Elizabethan world-picture, her lineage and connections made her a legitimate claimant for the English throne. She was the only child of James V, King of Scotland; her paternal grandmother was Henry VIII's sister, and her mother Marie of Guise was sister to the King of France.

[6]   Summit (1996), p. 412. Other recent readers raise questions about both Mary's aptitude for and interest in espionage. Holmes writes that, at least in the early years of her imprisonment, Mary's correspondence and even her plotting center around obtaining release or easing the conditions of her imprisonment. Occasionally Mary's writings touch on Scottish affairs or mention her son, but rarely at the early stages do we find Catholic proselytizing or any interest in unseating Elizabeth.

Mary was under Shrewsbury's watch from 1569 to 1584; Sir Ralph Sadler assumed the job from 1584 until 1585, and Sir Amyas Paulet took over later in 1585, supervising Mary's care until her execution in February 1586. She was 44 when she was beheaded, having spent nearly two decades, and most of her adult life, in prison.

third husband and reputed murderer of her second, Henry Stuart, Lord Darnley. Copies of Mary's sonnets and letters were presented by a group of Scottish lords at a 1568–1569 enquiry of the English council, convened to determine Mary's involvement in Darnley's death and pass sentence upon her. Used against her, Mary's poetry appears to expose secrets about her private life along with the liabilities of her official position.

Relations between the two queens and cousins have frequently been rendered by the petty language of rivalry and jealousy, and their letters often appear to draw on the raw discourse of insinuation and insult. Yet early modern women's relations are never wholly personal, as we have already seen; such a reading confines women to a narrow world they never inhabited and rude language they never spoke. In truth, the two queens, Maureen Quilligan (2006) likewise observes, "may have had more sympathy and understanding for each other than we have supposed" (para 2), both "subject to the political difficulties inherent in female rule." Mary's letters to Elizabeth, to Elizabeth's secretary of state William Cecil, and to Catholic supporters during the period of early captivity (1568–1571), for instance, reflect a complex pattern of threats and retreats. In a 1569 letter to Elizabeth, for example, she forswears authorship of incriminating letters with the odd statement that she has "never written such silly things, even if [she] had imagined them" (*Letters*, p. 170). In another letter, Mary emphasizes her good will towards Elizabeth's advisors, not only out of "respect to my said good sister" but, pointedly reminding them of her own claim to the throne, "because I am so nearly allied to [Elizabeth] in blood" (*Letters*, p. 172). And, in a 1568 statement presented by Mary's commissioners, she firmly insists on her royal power by offering a bathetic image of her demise: "As to the abdication of my crown, concerning which you have written to me, I beg you will trouble me no more on that point; for I am resolved and determined to die sooner than do so; and the last word which I shall utter in this life shall be that of a Scottish Queen" (*Letters* p. 167). Mary's artistry during this early period reveals a similar ambivalence about her royal position, but I also find in it a more carefully prepared legal–even sovereign–assumption of entitlement.

Many scholars have argued that women's needlework and their writings, at least in the early modern period, are entirely different expressive vehicles, utterly at odds in representing women's voices and their abilities. A joint examination of Mary Stuart's needlework and poetry leads me to disagree. As we saw in Chapter 1, needlework was a prescribed activity for aristocratic and middle-class women in the early modern period, primarily valued for the silence and obedience it fostered since busy hands would stifle unruly thoughts. Virgilia's reclusiveness only underscores this: needlework is not creative because it is not procreative; indeed, Shakespeare's version of Penelope in *Coriolanus* is a female double of her fearsome husband, without pity or real feeling. In contrast, Petrarchan sonneteering offered the male poet the means to demonstrate his passion and mastery (Vickers, p. 99). The poet-lover idealized his lady, praising the beauty of his beloved's body piece-by-piece, her dismembered form finally a testament to his wit and power. To pick up the needle was thus to lay down the pen, to become the mute image of femininity male poets celebrated, an image always available and empty. Margaret Cavendish will later represent the conflict in her poetry, confessing her preference "to write with the pen [rather] than to work with a needle."[7] Anne Finch similarly explains her rebellion against needlework: "My hand delights to trace unusual things, / And deviates from the known and common way" (cited by Parker and Pollock, p. 66).

But somehow both practices speak for Mary Stuart in captivity, and not merely in complementary ways—just as her long suffering and eventual execution might at once signify Elizabeth's power over a criminal, even a royal one, and further Mary's own political importance as Catholic queen. The ambiguities surrounding Mary's detainment in England remained useful to Elizabeth for many years,[8] but the unusual possibilities found in such deprivation and privacy were valuable to Mary, too. The symbols Mary employs to represent her plight can be deeply personal or highly stylized, both raw and overcooked, expressive sometimes of sheer feeling, at other times of cautious politicking. Yet at bottom Mary's needlework and poetry symbolize each other in mythologizing her power and her powerlessness, her passivity and passion. Her considerable energy, craft, and cunning supplying a way to shore up scattered loyalties and dismantle political obstacles while providing a rival image of a queen whose capacity to rule is tied up with her ability to forswear it. Materializing the business of state, Mary delineates a royal setting utterly unlike Elizabeth's court, articulated through a language of sexuality, maternity, sacrifice, unapologetic desire, and intermittent ambition, along with a theory of queenship as intimately connected to the labors of the household.

***

Early modern women's needlework has been the subject of much scrutiny by literary scholars, with little real consensus. In part, the problem is that the end-product (at once belittled and admired through adjectives like "elaborate," "precious," or "fine") and the process (where adjectives like "tedious," "decorative," or "mechanical" divorce the skill from any art or thought) appear to have so little in common. Moreover, during the early modern period, the process was becoming more important than the product, as the rules and behaviors codifying femininity became more significant than anything women might do or think.

There were notable exceptions, and Mary Stuart's work—all of it supremely functional and completed in a limited range of stitches (see Swain, 1973, p. 121)— nicely illustrates the point. At the very end of Margaret Swain's 1973 study of Mary's needlework, for instance, there is a picture of a set of child's reins said to have been embroidered by Mary for James VI, the child she would never again see

---

[7] *A True Relation of My Birth, Breeding, and Life* (1656). Excerpted by Travitsky and Prescott.

[8] Mary's unusual position was useful to Elizabeth because it afforded the Tudor queen the twinned chance to monitor a rival and safeguard a blood relation. She protected Mary's royal blood as long as it threatened her own, as long as her own status at home and on the world's stage seemed fragile.

after fleeing Scotland in 1568, leaving her two-year-old son to learn to walk and ride without her (pp. 86, 122). The gift is a beautiful one, in red silk (now faded to pink) with gold and silver thread and a Latin inscription carefully spelled out ("Angelis Svis Devs Mandavit De Te Vt Cvstodiant Te In Omnibvs Viis Tvis"), a gorgeous if solemn present for a motherless king more or less supervised by Mary's foes, including James's godmother Elizabeth.[9] But was this present simply one of many with which the frustrated (and often sickly) queen busied herself, the "product" of "long years of inactivity," as Francis de Zulueta describes them (p. 5)? Was her gift to James a way to send him a message, or a rich substitute for one? We have already seen that Renaissance gifts were nearly always nuanced and meticulously calculated. In addition to the New Year's gifts aristocratic women offered to their queen, one thinks of the pair of gloves Mary would present to a member of the Dayrell family on the morning of her execution, an extravagance that a powerful queen or condemned prisoner might equally, easily afford (Jourdain, p. 43), or of the jeweled pin fashioned into a whip, which poet and courtier Philip Sidney presented to Elizabeth in 1581. Such gifts beg a similar question: Are they lavish shows of strength or submission?

A related question is whether Mary's needlework is evidence of boredom or misery, aesthetic aspiration or political ambition, and thus whether it undermines queenly power or advances it. Common knowledge is that Elizabeth abandoned needlework when she assumed the throne in 1558, although she apparently continued the activity into adulthood,[10] long enough at least to have embroidered a cushion on display at Windsor Castle (Digby, p. 108). Princess Elizabeth was clearly proficient at needlework, and we know of the eleven-year-old's translation of *The Miroir or Glasse of the Synneful Soul* along with other gifts for her brother and father.[11] Needlework and literary accomplishments worked hand-in-hand to bolster Elizabeth's uneasy political position in her father's court.

Mary Stuart's early needlework in the French court of Henry II was undertaken with more confidence and tender support. Not only was she betrothed at the age of

---

[9] In *Needlework*, Swain (1973) translates the inscription as "God hath given his angels charge over thee: to keep thee in all thy ways." "Each word," Swain notes, "is separated by a sceptre, lion, swaddled infant, or heart, each surmounted by a crown" (p. 86). No doubt the exiled Mary wanted to remind James not to discount any of the various angels God had provided for her son's care.

[10] Frye (1999) maintains that Elizabeth "[left] behind her needlework with her disempowered youth" (pp. 167–9). Cf. *The Needles Excellency* (1629?) where John Taylor celebrates needlework as a pastime of queens, including Mary and Elizabeth Tudor. I thank Mihoko Susuki for this reference.

[11] See Jourdain's account (p. 41); Klein's (1997) treatment of Elizabeth's gift-giving (pp. 462, 476–7); and Frye (1999, p. 167). Connections between royal reading and embroidery are not unusual; Benoist Garroust, Mary's embroiderer in Scotland, also reportedly produced the velvet casings for many of the books in her library, as Durkan reports (p. 72).

54   *Women's Wealth and Women's Writing in Early Modern England*

five to the dauphin Francois, but she had also been crowned the queen of Scotland before her first birthday. Like Elizabeth, Mary was trained in Italian and Latin as well as in dance and embroidery and dress-making, noblewomen's accomplishments also practiced by Catherine de Medici and her husband's mistress Diane de Poitiers. Both Mary's and Elizabeth's varied careers in and out of favor also reflect the confines and possibilities of female courtly space as something private yet political, domestic by default.[12] Gradually, private space would become more and more linked to, and explained by, the habits and inhabitants of the household. But Elizabeth's privy chamber continued to serve as a powerful political space, so that her concealment was an elaborate and intensely public activity.[13] For Mary, private space would increasingly come to be identified with everything the court was not—a jail cell, a sickroom, a lair for popish plots, a closely-monitored workroom—a world created by isolation, deprivation, silence, paranoia, and boredom. Indeed, the French ambassador's account of Mary's confinement reads like something out of an early modern conduct book justifying woman's place in the home: "She is more happy and safe in her captivity, if she did but know it, than with more liberty, seeing that her mind could not rest long enough without getting into mischief."[14]

***

The recent editors of Elizabeth's collected literary works convincingly maintain that her "identity as princess and monarch cannot be separated from her identity as author."[15] Yet Mary Stuart's love poetry deliberately strives to make such a separation, while her needlework just as painstakingly proclaims her political ambitions and presumption. Perhaps one reason for the difference between Mary's and Elizabeth's artistry can be proposed at the outset. According to Janel Mueller, Elizabeth "did not regard her feminine gender as clearly or rigorously mandating what she must do or be;" whereas Mary frequently relied on gender as an excuse or explanatory rubric, as I aim to demonstrate here (see Mueller, 2000, pp. 221–2). I also want to consider what the final shape of Mary's collected works might look like, as a self-contradictory corpus not unlike their maker's almost phantasmagoric shape.

This project has obstacles we almost immediately encounter. One is the complicated, sometimes hysterical mythology surrounding Mary, with confusions over whether to see her as Catholic martyr or harmless papist plotter, pathetic exile

---

[12]   See Starkey (pp. 1–9). That both Elizabeth and Mary were esteemed for their poetry by their contemporaries is something to which recent critics draw our attention: see Summit (1996, 2000), and Herman (2002), who interestingly observes that Mary's poetry (unlike Elizabeth's) has received little critical attention because "both Mary and her work transect a number of national literatures without precisely belonging to any."

[13]   See Elizabeth Brown's (1999) discussion of Elizabeth's female courtiers and kinship connections (pp. 131–2). A related discussion of the privy chamber is provided by Knowles.

[14]   Castelnau de Mauvissiere's 1581 letter to Henry III is quoted by Batho (p. 4).

[15]   See the editors' preface to Elizabeth I's *Collected Works*, especially pp. xii–xiii.

or whore of Babylon.[16] A second difficulty surrounding much of Mary's poetry and needlework alike is the unclear nature of their authorship or origins: whether, for example, the embroidery belongs instead to the hand of Bess or to the members of Bess's household, or whether the love poems (which have no originals) were actually commissioned by the head of Elizabeth's spy ring Francis Walsingham, perhaps even forged by George Buchanan (James's Protestant tutor) to establish Mary's guilt in Darnley's death.[17] This "problem" of authorship is, however, common to many women's works of the period, typically jointly produced, edited, and circulated. Like Mary's reliance upon conventional tent stitches, her choice of the sonnet form both obscures features of her artistry and clarifies the dimensions of her talents.

At once textual, political, and gendered, many of the problems surrounding Mary's work illustrate the need for and rhyme of a "female poetics"—something which Elizabeth's works over and over again magnificently obscure (see Fleming, p. 204). The instability of Mary's works is one of the signs of these poetics; according to Juliet Fleming, such work is typically of "doubtful transmission [;]" it is "not spoken from the position of a unified subject" and, more than likely, "it does not speak oppositionally" (p. 204). These "female poetics" suggest the most promising way to relate Mary's use of symbols from such different registers. If Mary's needlework and poetry are elements of a missing autobiography, they also offer us keys to the ways that many early modern women could explore their ties and their powers.

***

Typically viewed as a form of "busy-work" for noblewomen and necessary housework for lower-class women, needlework may be the most public and visible thing about the famously closeted Mary, hardly, then, an instrument of withdrawal or suppression. But, in many other ways, needlework of the early modern period seems simultaneously important and unimportant. Lena Cowen Orlin (1999) describes needlework as supplying a strategy or "construct" of invisibility, manufacturing concrete evidence that a woman will not speak. In upholding silence (and thereby chastity, as early modern thinkers reasoned), needlework

---

[16] See Lynch's account of some of the historiographical problems in his Introduction.

[17] See Bax's translation of The *Letters and Poems of Mary Stuart, Queen of Scots* (p. 6). While I consult Bax's translation, I rely on a more recent one provided by Herman (2002), in part because of its emphasis on the role of Jane Gordon, something I explore later in this chapter. The Casket letters and sonnets (referred to in this way because they were allegedly found in a silver casket in the possession of Bothwell) failed to seal Mary's guilt, and Elizabeth would wait another 18 years before sentencing Mary to death, not for Darnley's murder but for conspiring to depose Elizabeth. Mary Burke (2000) summarizes the textual history (pp. 101–2). Most scholars believe the much more damning Casket letters that accompanied the sonnets are fakes.

serves as a "talisman of virtue,"[18] so that it is less a symbol-making activity than a symbol of inactivity.

During the middle ages, however, male as well as female professionals were often celebrated for their embroidery, and the Broderers Guild, reconstituted in 1561, was presided over by a set of male officials (Parker and Pollock, p. 60). But the iconoclasm of the Reformation meant that needlework was increasingly undertaken for secular rather than sacred purposes. Embroidered altar cloths and priestly vestments were often turned into draperies or bedspreads, like the altar cloths Mary Stuart proposed to employ in Bothwell's apartments or the materials she and Bess recycled in the Oxburgh hangings (See Swain, 1973, p. 51; Ellis, p. 284).[19] The magnificent work of the middle ages known as Opus Anglicanum ("English work"), with silver-gilt thread, seed pearls and semi-precious stones, was replaced after the Reformation by needlework produced for the home and the person, for clothing and furniture; it became a "quotidian practice" which decorated rather than obliterated the everyday.[20] Chapter 5 takes up the care and furnishing of Bess's households in greater detail, because her own continued efforts at magnificence link domesticity with control and retirement with power in ways that help us grasp both the "tumultuous energies" of the household and the authority early modern women wielded within it (Wall, 2002, pp. 7–8).

But at the very same time that the household was becoming increasingly complex and conflicted, "the art of embroidery, once the most valued cultural form of medieval ecclesiastical culture," was, Griselda Pollock argues, becoming "progressively deprofessionalised, domesticated, and feminised" (p. 25; see also Parker and Pollock, p.59 ff.). Mary, in fact, was working at a time when embroidery was becoming simultaneously domesticated and secularized, and thereby rendered amateurish. More than that, needlework had seemingly become a household chore as well as a categorical imperative of gender, "consigned to a special category" as women's work and "seen simply as [a] homogeneous [expression] of 'femininity'" (Parker and Pollock, p. xviii). This development of feminine "crafts" may explain why women's artwork is typically viewed as a conflict between self-indulgence and serious commitment, never harmoniously both. A similar perspective allows

---

[18] Citing needlework's "quasi-magical property," Orlin (1999) suggests it can function "less as a charm than as a cloak, a cloak that obscures, that wraps Annabella in irreproachable activity, that shields her from the penetrating gaze of her father, and that disguises her subversive intents" (pp. 183–4). Perhaps Orlin's emphasis on needlework as shielding what women are really doing also enables her to refer to Mary Stuart as "that obsessive needlewoman" (p. 189).

[19] See Swain (1973, p.51); Ellis (p. 284). Further analysis of the impact of Reformation iconoclasm is provided by Kendrick.

[20] See Fumerton's discussion of the poetics of everyday life in her introduction; and Wilson for a discussion of "the female quotidian."

"Manifest Housekeepers" 57

many scholars, as Lawrence Lipking notes, to comment that the poems of a woman writer tend to be written "despite herself."[21]

The artist is an unfortunate casualty of her art, according to such a sentimental critical model. I want instead to take up another possibility, one raised by more recent readers of women's work. Throughout her life, as Susan Frye (1999) tells us, Mary used needlework to fashion the "visually emblematic counterpoint to her authorship of letters and poetry" (p. 170). One might push Frye's claims harder still, for needlework supplies Mary with an eloquent and forceful means to proclaim and bolster her extraordinary lineage, her claims to legitimacy, and her powerful position on the European stage. If it is a consoling gesture, Mary's needlework is also a symptom of intense preoccupation and a vehicle for important state business. This is especially true in the most famous examples of Mary's needlework.

During her first few years under the care of the Earl of Shrewsbury and his wife, Mary and Bess planned, designed, and embroidered the four Oxburgh hangings.[22] Each of the three large hangings and fragment of a fourth—all of green velvet— displays a square centerpiece surrounded by octagonal panels of emblematic subjects, along with Mary's cipher in several places. Familiar emblems, worked in the relatively easy tent stitches (or petit point), include Mary's chief impresa, a hand holding a pruning hook trimming a vine, and a marigold turning to the sun (the impresa of Margaret of Valois, Mary's sister-in-law) with the Latin motto Non inferiora secutus ("Not following lower things"). These are the most recurrent and provocative of Mary's symbols. The marigold emblem was also used for the cushion cover Mary worked for Elizabeth, where she included the inscription "Sa virtue m'Atire ("Its strength draws me"), an anagram for Marie Stuart (and possible reference to the many images with which Mary could attire herself).[23] Other emblems in the Oxburgh hangings include a palm tree and crawling tortoise (referring to her second marriage to the uncrowned Darnley), a phoenix (the emblem of her mother Marie of Guise), a dragon, a unicorn, a sea moonke, a leopard, an ape, an elephant, and a paired dolphin (the pun on "Dauphin" refers to Mary's first marriage to Francois), and "she-dolphin."

In the course of preparing a catalog of impresas and emblems, William Drummond would later write to Ben Jonson about another one of Mary's alleged works, an embroidered bed intended for James.[24] Drummond's description nicely underscores the sweep and range of Mary's vision of herself, articulated through an emblematic language that is remarkably familiar and accessible and at the same time highly charged:

---

[21] See Lipking's discussion of Mary's contemporary, the poet Gaspara Stampa (pp. 170–75).

[22] I draw primarily on Swain's (1973) account (pp. 95–119), but see also de Zulueta and Digby. Additional details about the hangings' sources, techniques, significance as furnishings, and Bess's involvement are provided by Ellis.

[23] I thank an anonymous reader of the book-manuscript for this suggestion.

[24] Swain (1973) reports that the piece is now missing (p. 90).

Fig. 3.1   A hand with a pruning knife, with the motto *Virescit Vulnere Virtus* and the Royal Arms of Scotland

I have been curious to find out for you the Impresaes and Emblems on a Bed of State wrought and embroidered all with gold and silk by the late Queen Mary . . . the first is the Loadstone turning towards the pole, the word her Majesties name turned on an Anagram, Maria Stuart, *sa virtu m'attire*, This hath reference to a Crucifix, before which with all her Royall ornaments she is humbled on her knees most lively, with the word, undique, an Impresa of Mary of Lorrain, her Mother, a Phoenix in flames, the word, *en ma fin git mon commencement* [in my end is my beginning]. . . . TheImpressa of Henry the second, the French King, a Cressant, the word *Donec totum impleat orbem* [Till he fills the whole world]. The Impressa of King Francis the first, a Salamander crowned in the midst of Flames, the word, *Nutrisco et extinguo*.

The images of twinned queens are particularly pronounced in this work, as are references to Mary's French relations, royal connections, and papal ties:

Two Women upon the Wheels of Fortune, the one holding a Lance, the other a Cornucopia; which Impressa seemeth to glaunce at Queen Elizabeth and herself . . . . The Impressa of the Cardinal of Lorrain her Uncle, a Pyramid overgrown with ivy. . . a ship with her Mast broken and fallen in the Sea . . . . This is for herself and her Son, a big Lyon, and a young Whelp beside her . . . . The Impressa of King Henry the eight, a Portculles . . . . The Impressa of the Duke of Savoy, the annunciation of the Virgin Mary . . . . Flourishes of Armes, as Helmes, Launces, Corslets, Pikes, Muskets, Canons . . . . Ecclipses of the Sun and Moon . . . glauncing, as may appear, at Queen Elizabeth. Brennus Ballances, a sword cast in to weigh gold . . . . A Trophie upon a Tree, with Mytres, Crowns, Hats, Masks, Swords, Books, and a Woman with a Vail about her eyes, or muffled, pointing to some about her.[25]

Drummond's annotations are useful in reading the Oxburgh hangings as well, because they likewise illustrate Mary's supreme confidence in her genealogy. In the confines of the Shrewsbury quarters, she—with not a little help from Bess—had fashioned an imperial cosmology, a royal explanatory apparatus vast, beautiful, and prophetic. The divine predictions are exhibited too in the cushion she made for the Duke of Norfolk in 1569 with her arms, the motto *Virescit Vulnere Virtus* ("Virtue flourishes by wounding") and, once more, the image of a hand holding a pruning knife, cutting down a vine. Margaret Swain and others have argued that Mary was alerting Norfolk that her position would be strengthened with the removal of Elizabeth's inferior claim and sterile line. There were several plots involving marriage between Mary and Norfolk, secretly aligned with Catholic Spain, and the cushion was introduced at Norfolk's trial for treason. Apparently everyone knew how to read past or through Mary's artifice.

---

[25]   This account is drawn from de Zulueta (pp. 5–6); it is reprinted by Jourdain (pp. 149–51).

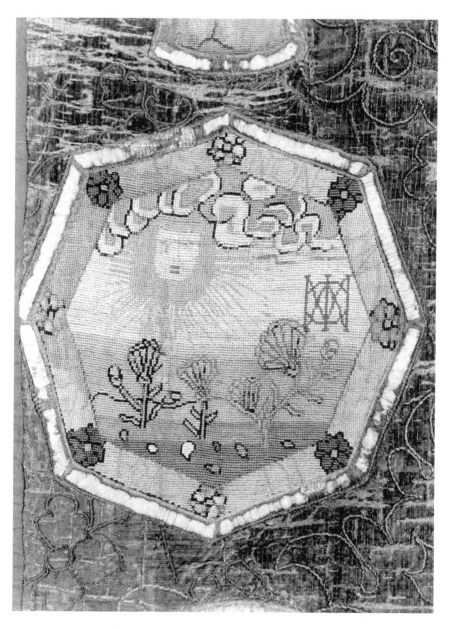

Fig. 3.2   Marigold turning to the sun, with the motto *Non Inferiora Secutus* and Mary Stuart's cipher.

The rest of Mary's embroidered images of tigers, flowers, planets, fish and beasts in the Oxburgh hangings are nearly all derived from designs provided by contemporary herbiaries, emblem books, physician's texts, and mythological narratives—rather than from Catholic iconography, something particularly striking in view of Mary's important status as Catholic queen (however devout she may have been in reality). The sea moonke panel depicts a monster, for instance, that would have been especially repellent to Protestants. But blatantly Catholic symbols or even overtly biblical narratives would have diminished Mary's role as a reader of Elizabeth's narrative, a story that cast the English queen as Mary's defective predecessor, and the New World as the site of Mary's throne. Like other early modern women who "plied the needle to materialize [their] views of the world and to be remembered as makers of objects that commemorated themselves [and] their families" (Jones and Stallybrass, p. 170), there is an artful duality insistently operating in all of Mary's embroidery, subduing the aggression in her threats while dramatizing her passivity. It makes her rebellion lawful, pious, and eminently queenlike.

***

Because of the more conventional origins and collaborative production of Mary's needlework, it seems difficult to manufacture out of it the "heroic narrative" of self-definition typically produced by the corpus of a painter or sculptor.[26] Mary's needlework does supply a self-narrative, however. Unlike Elizabeth's shrewd calculation of her gender as something "virtual" in her speeches—a set of attributes she might draw on or ignore, given her royal position, to suit her royal position— Mary's needlework frequently emphasizes how the stereotypically feminine roles of wife and mother and daughter enable her to assume and discharge the office, qualities and responsibilities of a monarch. Even her image of the milkmaid and reindeer conflates a lower-class chore with this sovereign power. Elizabeth may have resorted at times to an image of herself as mother to her country, but Mary sees herself over and over again as mother and wife and daughter to a legitimate line of rulers (see Mueller, 2000, p. 223).

---

[26] In the past, scholars like Nevinson described the lack of artistry (or originality) in Mary's needlework, since embroiderers typically relied upon or even copied patterns out of herbiaries. As Nevinson maintains, the "ability to use the pencil and pen does not necessarily go with ability to use the needle. Mary Queen of Scots was the most celebrated needlewoman of her day, but during her imprisonment in Lochleven Castle in 1567 she petitioned the Lords of the Scottish Council for five servants, one of whom was to be 'an imbroderer to drawe forthe such worke as she would be occupied about'" (pp. xv–xvi).

Silvers explains some of the other "problems" associated with female artistry: "Not all art is equally amenable to being situated in heroic narrative, for the makers of some sorts of works, for instance, African carvings, medieval manuscript illuminations, ethnic dance, and quilts, usually go undocumented. . . . For other kinds of objects, like ceramics or textiles, the canon itself is structured in terms of periods or styles rather than of individual artists of even individual master works" (p. 376).

Fig. 3.3   Mary Stuart's Sea Moonke

Susan Frye (1999) claims the needlework produced during Mary's imprisonment "constitute[s] ciphers of her political identity and consequent ambition." This is because needlework provided Mary with a platform to explain her invisibility along with an opportunity to "[sew] herself into a web of referents to her rank, marital connection, exile, and imprisonment under Elizabeth I" (pp. 170, 174). Women's work becomes a crucial instrument of courtly intervention, just as Princess Elizabeth's gift to Parr was an acknowledgment of and experiment upon all of the links between them. Mary's designs more fully empty needlework of any conventional meanings. Her calculated combination of familiar emblems and royal ciphers challenges the dominant codes at work in needlework, disrupting its standard iconography to produce personal and political meanings all her own, ones that exploit her singularity even as she explains and erases it. Unlike the bastard Elizabeth, Mary's queenly identity was always premised on linkages to others. One historian goes as far as to call Mary "a highly complex dynastic prodigy, almost a monstrosity, related to, and a threat to, many families" (Merriman, p. 48).

My emphasis, though, is on Mary's prodigious work. My reading of it conflicts with Lena Cowen Orlin's 1999 account of women's needlework that emphasizes its passivity and minimizes its artistry as well as its aggression. As Orlin argues:

> The busy-ness of fancy stitchery was a cultural myth, intended to suggest to women of status that their practice of embroidery was in some sense comparable to (and as valuable as) the professional and profit-making pursuits of men. Even the term "needlework," so often shortened to just "work" in the language of the time, was collusive in this cultural construct. It implied a priority interest in the product, when in fact that which was necessary to the gender hierarchy was the process. (p. 191)

Mary's work teaches us something rather different about women, their status, and their work, however. If Elizabeth was a "portable queen," for instance, whose reign was marked by "continuing ceremonial dialogue" and a peripatetic existence,[27] Mary's inert and hidden state appears just as intrinsic to her political and imaginative role, for she fights battles, woos courtiers, wins the sympathies and not infrequent consternation of popes, all from a distant place of retirement. Moreover, the works she produces under lock and key are less an effort to obtain release than to represent the salutary or admonitory effect of her withdrawal on her audience. Mary's images in the Oxburgh hangings in particular illustrate the history and meaning of her captive status and its moral significance. They also provide fantastical pictures of a vast new world in contrast with–but not inferior to–the universe presided over by Elizabeth, of an Eden populated by toucans, leopards, ferrets, and two queens, cousins who might replace Adam and Eve, or supersede Cain and Abel.

---

[27] Cole writes that Elizabeth's visits to over 400 individual and civic hosts were "emblematic of her rule and intrinsic to her ability to govern" (p. 1).

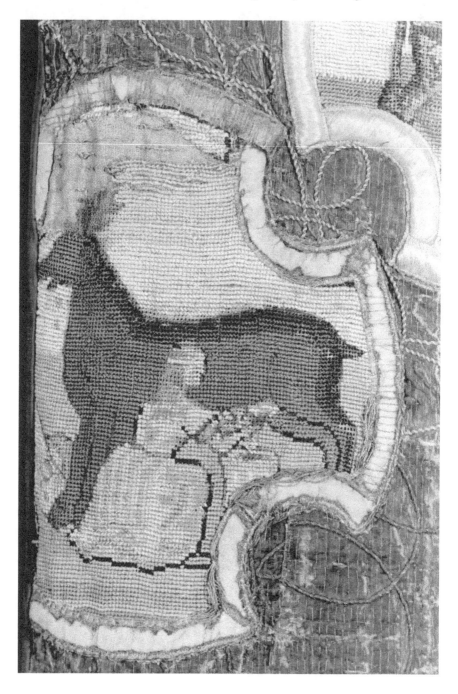

Fig. 3.4　　Mary Stuart's Reindeer and Milkmaid

***

Mary Stuart's oeuvre is also a useful reminder to literary scholars that female passivity can merely seem quiescent. Indeed, both her needlework and her sonnets constitute an anticipatory poetics, or what Ann Rosalind Jones (1986) calls a "pre"-poetics, an expressive technique which lays the groundwork "necessary for [any] writing at all" (p. 74). These "pre"-poetics seem equally appropriate to a prisoner on death row, a royal successor, a houseguest in transit, or the other woman in a love affair. All of these uneasy positions describe Mary at one point or another during her short life. Over and over in her works, Mary explicitly yearns to replace the context of or alter the audience for the messages she sends: seeking a meeting with Elizabeth that would never transpire, for instance, or a divorce for Bothwell so that Mary might marry the man she alleged had kidnapped and raped her. Jane Marcus provides another way to read these efforts, describing women's work in terms of a transformational aesthetic, a "model of art, with repetition and dailiness at the heart of it" (p. 84), a set of material practices offered not in resistance or concession to a male reality but as a means of transmitting female culture and its values.

To take Mary's work seriously is thus to acknowledge all of its concessions and contradictions and manipulations of her freedom and captivity. It also means reading her needlework and poetry together, a rather difficult enterprise, as I keep suggesting. For if Mary's needlework aims to remind Elizabeth of Mary's sovereign claims while undermining those of her cousin, Mary's sonnets to Bothwell challenge the idea that a queen really has any power at all, except a power to relinquish. As Mary writes in sonnet 2:

> Into his hands and absolute power
> I place my son, my honor and my life,
> My country, my subjects, my subjected soul
> Are all for him, and I have no other desire
> For my object than, without deceit,
> To follow him, despite all the suffering
> That may follow. Because I have no other wish
> But to make him perceive that my faithfulness,
> Whatever storm or good weather that comes,
> Will never change its house or place. (Herman ed., lines 1–10).

This sonnet sequence, originally written in French—and allegedly written to James Hepburn, the earl of Bothwell—has long been controversial; and the details of production and circulation are as complicated as those surrounding the needlework. Darnley was murdered in February of 1567, and Mary remarried three months later after an apparently collusive abduction in April of that year. The sonnets, if they are hers, would seem to date from this disturbed period just before or after Darnley's death, when she was awaiting reassurances from her

66   *Women's Wealth and Women's Writing in Early Modern England*

lover and from the Scottish nobles, some of whom would rally behind Mary, others of whom rebelled and forced her to surrender in June.[28] But the political crisis pales next to the erotic uncertainty Mary faces in her poems: her position as queen of Scotland is jeopardized not because of civil unrest but because of unrequited affection. This is a reversal of the way courtiers like Sidney employed love poetry to "metamorphize rivalry" among themselves, according to Arthur Marotti—although such a practice emerged, Marotti notes, in the latter part of Queen Elizabeth's reign (pp. 396–7), long after the equivocal appearance of Mary's sonnets. Mary's poems, in contrast, explicitly downplay politics in favor of other contests. Before the marriage to Bothwell could take place, an expedited divorce from Jane Gordon, Lady Bothwell, had to be obtained. Without a marriage to sanctify their love (or reward a plot to murder Darnley), Mary appears strangely paralyzed, but the sonnets picture for us a queen who again and again wishes to remind us that she's a woman and, for that reason, powerless.[29]

If Mary's needlework boldly announces the claims of maternity and genealogy over the rulings of the English state, there is a conflict between external and internal forces in the sonnets, something which also forms much of their subject matter. Male lovers since Petrarch were able to make the beloved's powers their own: praising her eyes or heart or breasts, they fashioned out of their gaze a poetic identity that made female beauty an instrument rather than a snare. Female sonneteers drew then on tools and images and habits meant to disable women. Rarely did women's love poetry turn the tables on the male beloved or on

---

[28]   Tutored in poetry by Ronsard, Mary wrote sonnets as a girl; but some readers, including Antonia Fraser and Ronsard himself, reject the sonnets as Mary's work. Donaldson suggests that the documents were made out of an "amalgam of letters, some by Mary to Bothwell, some by Mary but not to Bothwell, some to Bothwell but not by Mary" (p. 73; quoted by Mary Burke [2000] p. 102 n2). Along with Travitsky (1981), Burke (2000), and Hanson, I take the sonnets to be Mary's, mostly because the sonnets are not incriminating in and of themselves and forgeries would better aim to establish evidence of Mary's guilt in or knowledge of Darnley's murder. For additional support of this reasoning, see Bax (p. 8) and Travitsky (1981, pp. 188–9).

Others have supported the idea of Mary's authorship because of the fact that her court, particularly during the period of the courtship and marriage to Darnley, was apparently the inspiration for the bulk of the Bannatyne Manuscript of 1568, a comprehensive anthology of late Scots medieval poetry (see Lynch, p. 15).

[29]   Mary Burke (2000) reads this inertia as a symptom of Stuart's "poetic cross-dressing," something which "results in an uneasy conjunction of expressions of dominance and extreme passivity, which parallels attempts in her own life to balance the demands of being a monarch and woman" (pp.102–3); Burke cites as another example of this "cross-dressing" Mary's use of feminine occupations like needlework at council meetings "to dispel anxiety over the sight of a woman exercising power" (p. 111). Burke's account is very suggestive, but I think it over-emphasizes the willed nature of Mary's paralysis; it also elides Elizabeth's similar problems as female queen, as well as the fact that Mary's own mother governed Scotland as regent for almost 19 years.

Petrarchan habits: Mary Wroth's *Pamphilia* never, for instance, exacts revenge on her inconstant lover. Instead, female poets often turn the dismembering gaze on themselves. As Diana E. Henderson observes, when female poets complained, they "called attention to their lack of education and access to language, and deprecated their ability as a result; however, literary genres per se were not perceived as the sources of inhibition."[30]

Mary Stuart's poetry seems to fit this characterization, too, providing her with the opportunity to abandon politics altogether rather than "to take on a masculine role and its powers and/or to modify them so that they capture experiences and values perceived as feminine." Mary explains her abjection as abdication in the first sonnet:

> For him I value all my friends as less than nothing
> And of my enemies I hope well.
> I have risked for him fame and conscience:
> I would for him renounce the world:
> I would die to advance him. (Herman ed., lines 9–13)

This announcement is not as starkly "deprecating" as Henderson might indicate, however. We have already seen in examining her needlework how Mary often explores the elastic, even fictive, quality of queenly powers. Marotti describes the "imaginative heterocosms within which ambitious men could fantasize a kind of mastery they lacked in their actual experience" (p. 398); in stark contrast, Mary suggests that she will confine herself to a domestic sphere if it enables her to express most fully her vast powers and overwhelming love. The real irony is that Mary pledges to invent a private realm or command a state of deprivation to please her lover, creating a state of exile at home which she would deplore in England just a few months later.

It seems easy for some critics to fault Mary for her erotic susceptibility or even for her mediocre poetry.[31] But given Mary's repeated experimentation with the limits and resources of her royal position, I think we should resist this kind of judgment, just as we should challenge the seemingly necessary antagonism between women's household labors and their literary endeavors, an antagonism which encourages Lawrence Lipking to posit the figure of the abandoned woman as the female artist par excellence—someone with no house to oversee, no state over which to preside, a poetics where Sappho obscures Penelope. Jane Marcus comments on Lipking's "tragic essentialism," explaining that "[t]he suffering posture of the abandoned woman is appealing to the phallic feminist because the absent male is at the center of the woman writer's text" (p. 82).

---

[30] Henderson (p. 46); see also pages 49–51 for an analysis of Mary's poetry.

[31] For an unusually nuanced discussion, see Hanson's exploration of the term "mediocre" (with its original meaning as "middling") as an appropriate one for the poetry of both Wroth and Stuart (p. 187).

Because Penelope remains at work in Mary's texts, we should also resist the image of Mary as overpowered by her blind love for Bothwell. (Similarly Marrotti comments on Sidney's "disingenuous overvaluation of love" [p. 402].) Like Mary Wroth, whose sonnets will appear more than 50 years later,[32] Mary Stuart clearly contrasts her constancy with the inconstancy of her lover. But Bothwell is often less interesting to Mary than is her rival, Jane Gordon; and Mary's self-narrative, with its anguished heroics, is offered in contrast to Lady Bothwell's inadequacies: "[H]e will know my constancy to be unfeigned, / Not by my tears or feigned obedience, not / As some other have done, but by various deeds" (Herman ed., 2 lines 12–14). In the next sonnet, Mary pledges, "she will not surpass me in this point" (Herman ed., 3 line 4). This world is fraught not with the dangers of scheming courtiers but with the debilitating confusions prompted by corrupt texts and faulty readers. If it has proven nearly impossible over the years to assign authorship of the sonnets entirely to Mary, it also remains unclear whether the poems are pleas for power, marriage, fidelity, or some acknowledgment of Mary's efforts as a writer or lover. Reminiscent of Goneril's jealousy of Regan in Shakespeare's *King Lear*, Mary's envy of Jane Gordon is raised throughout sonnet 3, where Mary revises the position and duties of a queen: "She, for her honor, owes you obedience. / I, in obeying you, can receive only blame, / not being, to my regret, like her, your wife" (3 lines1–3). In Clifford Bax's translation, Mary then laments, "[F]ine it is to queen it in your house; / Whereas what scandal doth my love arouse / Albeit she'll never serve you better than I!" (3 lines 6–8). "Queen" is the title Mary bestows on any woman who wins Bothwell's love or presides over his house. If Mary's envy of Lady Bothwell raises problems of literary agency and royal authority, it also suggests that Elizabeth's rival image took up only limited space in Mary's imagination.

Mary's erotic gaze and political anxieties are explicitly torn between two subjects in the sonnets. Her "firm constancy" (Herman ed., 7 line 2) for Bothwell puts all else at stake, and many times she reconfigures her royal power into fealty to her lover: "I have no wealth, happiness, or contentment, / Other than to obey him and to serve him loyally" (Herman ed., 8 lines 8–9). Bax's translations make the transfer of power more explicit: "Only to you, being subject . . . .To this I set my seal" (Bax ed., 11 lines 12, 14). But there is at the same time an overwhelming envy of and contempt for Bothwell's wife, someone whom Mary describes as haughty, "frigid" (Herman ed., 5 line 1), faithless (Herman ed., 3 line 14), base-born (Herman ed., 4 lines1–4), and a poor dresser (Herman ed., 5 lines 6–7). Mary even raises doubts about her rival's literary talents, describing Lady Bothwell in sonnet 6 as a poor writer who steals other's verse: "And she would now deceive my beloved / Through writings all painted with learning, / Which could not have come from her mind / But cribbed from some dazzling author" (Herman ed., lines 4–7). These suspicions are all the more disturbing when Mary tries to elicit Bothwell's love by denigrating her authority: "You think me a woman without judgment. /

---

[32] See Henderson (p. 51); Hanson draws a similar connection (pp. 179–83).

"*Manifest Housekeepers*" 69

And all this increases my passion" (7 lines 13–14).[33] It would be helpful to have Bothwell's sonnets in response, or any written record of feeling on his part; we tend to posit either unbridled lust or ambition in their absence, with little sense of how closely tied Mary and Bothwell might have been, both part of a larger social system that had already, John Guy insists, repeatedly put them together (pp. 304–6).

The absence of any such larger context makes the meaning and purposes of Mary's sonnets—which were hidden away, her accusers alleged, inside a silver casket—all the more unclear. Elizabeth Hanson refers to the "disastrously deauthorizing" "effect of the literary choices [Mary's sonnets] record."[34] Mary's choices of diction, image, and symbol are always instructive, but hardly "disastrous," I think; if their contradictions about her power and subjection as a queen and a lover are troubling, this ambivalence is basic structural principle of her needlework, too. The problem in the sonnets is that Mary's representation of her presumption or ambition is completely at odds with her queenly station, privileges or abilities. Sonnet 8, for example, concludes: "For him I await good fortune" (Herman ed., 8 line 10). With good reason Hanson describes this sonnet's "frantic impotence" (p.182); this is a bizarre capitulation, even for a "subjected soul" (Herman ed., 2 line 3) to make, yet it accords with the mythology Mary will later fabricate in the Oxburgh hangings.

We would read Mary's sonnets even were it not for their infamous application, because they are important examples of a woman's writing about herself as an agent and artist and lover all at once, someone who is also part of a larger erotic field crowded with other aspiring women, rival poets, and rival queens and objects of desire themselves. To be sure, Mary's sonnets employ a language of threats and pleas which bullies its readers with weakness, utterly unlike the careful and quiet positioning of patterns and meanings in Mary's embroidery, with its discourse of European and Latin tongues in possession of every trope. Mary's needlework afforded her—even in a prison not of her own making—with more vision and power and authority. But her poetry gave her scope to imagine a private realm where such power might best be enjoyed.

***

What happens to the spectacular picture of English Renaissance poetry—and to the equally gorgeous image of the poet inspired by his queen's celebrated image—when we shift our attention from Elizabeth to Mary? What happens when we turn from Elizabeth's imposing, "shaping" powers to those of Mary, who inspired so

---

[33] Herman (2002) describes Mary's jealousy of Jane Gordon, and comments that "[a]s much as Mary clearly despises her rival," she "still allows [Lady Bothwell] the same agency that she grants herself."

[34] Hanson (pp. 167, 179). For a study of Mary's son's authorizing choices in his poetry, see Herman (2001), who claims that "[f]or James, no discourse exists separate from sovereignty" (p. 1526).

70   *Women's Wealth and Women's Writing in Early Modern England*

many of Elizabeth's fears and much of Elizabeth's language?[35] Like Elizabeth, Mary is an extraordinary figure who provokes much of the imaginative discourse of the period; like her cousin, Mary was a female poet "neither silenced and marginalized nor oppositional in her writing, but rather one who occupie[d] the central position within Elizabethan culture." [36] But Mary is an exemplary figure as well, a person of privilege whose collected works indicate both power and defeat, subjugation and authority, whose defeat drove an Armada and whose desperate writings repeatedly forced Elizabeth into the position of desperate interpreter of Mary's story. Some of the contradictions in Mary's portrait are strategic, of course. They should make us question whether a queen like Mary can really opt to retire from her position. If Mary voluntarily chose passivity and assumed the voice of an uncrowned and unloved woman, we must wonder whether this is evidence of her cultural authority, or of Elizabeth's. In either case, Mary Stuart's artistry points to many of the issues a "female poetics" needs to consider. If in her poetry she redefines "queen" as ultimately a private person, a paradoxical position she was later pushed into as Elizabeth's guest, Mary's needlework redefines for us what women's work includes. Taken together, her artistry challenges any reading of women's work and its supposed "silences" by repeatedly highlighting the elusiveness of an "I" caught between erotic pressure and political paranoia, between self-doubt and grand deception. For all of these reasons, Mary Stuart's model is instructive for a reading of other early modern women's texts. Any of the "gaps" or "loud silences" in the production of women's texts might be explained, for one thing, with reference to women's other symbol-making activities, so that such gaps appear neither so wide nor so deep nor so disabling to critics (see Fleming, p. 201). Perhaps we also need to reevaluate what a woman's decision to write—or not to write—in the early modern period ultimately meant. Otherwise we run the risk of ignoring a literary problem that terrorized Mary's cousin Elizabeth for nearly 20 years.

---

[35]   In *The Art of English Poesie*, George Puttenham celebrates Elizabeth as "the greatest poet of all time," citing in particular her poem on Mary, "The Doubt of Future Foes." See Summit's (1996) discussion (p. 395 ff).

[36]   Summit (1996, p. 400). For more extended discussions of Mary's impact on Renaissance literature, see Phillips and Mazzola (2000).

Chapter 4
Strange Bedfellows

[W]ill it not please hir, by a letter of hir owne hand to commaund that which hir Majesty cannot commaund as my Souverain[e] but as my most honoured, loved and trusted kinswoman?[1]

Mary Stuart's education in France was "meticulously planned," according to biographer John Guy, with instruction in languages, philosophy, grammar, and the classics equivalent to the training the Dauphin, her betrothed, received—as well as lessons in dancing and needlework (p. 67). Yet there still was time for the young girl to play dress up and keep house with her Scottish companions, and Guy contrasts this harmless fun with some of Mary's later extravagances, especially her love of "sumptuous and expensive embroideries" that, even as a teenager, she purchased "indiscriminately." Against these baleful pleasures should be reckoned Mary's childhood pastimes, Guy maintains:

> On a more mundane level, Mary adored making cotignac, a type of French marmalade, putting on an apron and boiling quinces and sugar with powder of violets in a saucepan for hours before laying out the slices of crystallized fruits. The four Maries were all required to help her, and a mockup kitchen was created in their apartments so they could play at cooking and housekeeping, pretending to be servants or bourgeois women organizing their domestic routine and doing their own shopping. It was a game that Mary always remembered and sometimes played in Scotland, usually in St. Andrews, where she had a house near the abbey. (75–6)

That Mary's adult life as sovereign would be almost completely circumscribed by the "mundane" comforts and confinements of the household seems a strange irony, even a rude one, yet the parallel characterized the lives of many aristocratic women, seemingly schooled for intellectual pursuits and political conquest, yet moored to their families and the care of cloth, food, animals, and each other.[2]

---

[1] Arbella Stuart, Letter 16 to Sir Henry Brounker, taken from *The Letters of Lady Arbella Stuart*, edited by Steen (p. 160). Hereafter all references to Stuart's letters will be to this edition, and will be noted parenthetically in the text as Steen, *Letters*. For additional information about the material conditions surrounding the production and transmission of Stuart's letters, see Steen, "Manuscript Matters" (1994).

[2] For additional details, see Whitehead, ed.; and Pollock (1989). Although she focuses strictly on the early Tudor period, Harris (2002) offers valuable information about the important and challenging careers women undertook as wives.

72   *Women's Wealth and Women's Writing in Early Modern England*

Early modern housekeeping was anything but child's "play," however; and even in the Scottish queen's childhood "game" we find not nostalgia for a home the girl, sent to France at age five, never really had, but desire for a place where her considerable skills might be repeatedly tested and rewarded.

The prizes connected to the care of the early modern household could be extravagant ones too, and the stakes, despite Guy's characterization otherwise, extremely high. Indeed, the responsibilities were not reserved for "servants or bourgeois women," as Guy would have us see: twice Bess of Hardwick was charged by her queen to serve "as the guardian of a national and Christian stewardship," compelled to keep watch over two houseguests—one of them Mary Stuart—whom Elizabeth had committed to Bess's strict care for a decade in one case, sixteen years in another.[3] But such an awesome responsibility to maintain the household, even in the face of the most unruly elements of rebellion, immorality, and disorder, was something almost all early modern housewives regularly assumed; as Wendy Wall (2002) maintains, with women's fingers "on the pulse of life and death" and their energies devoted to "modes of disciplining," the household a "training ground for political order" comprising "the foremost disciplinary site in the period" (pp. 1, 3–4).

These responsibilities did not wane with the rise of a market economy in which "domestic work" could also involve financial dealings and contracted services (see Wall, 2002, p. 54); indeed, keeping one's proper place in such a porous and busy setting could prove a regular chore, too. Nor were these tasks only part of the middle-class household. Bolstered by the post-Reformation glorification of the household," Wall maintains, "even women of status took interest in the details of domestic labor" (p. 21) and she cites the examples of Lady Catherine Sedley, Lady Elizabeth Grey, Lady Elinor Fethplace, and Lady Grace Mildmay.

In this chapter I explore some of the varied meanings of the household for its early modern inhabitants, examining Bess's surveillance efforts alongside her granddaughter Arbella Stuart's elaborate labors to evade them. In a remarkable stream of letters produced in the long winter months of 1602–1603, Stuart attempts an escape, transacts marriage plans, and most significantly perhaps, asserts her powers and rights as a princess of the blood by explaining, over and over again, her position in the home. A "humble, and obediente childe" as well as a "discomfort" and "poore silly infant," Stuart represents herself, in addition, as a "branch" of Elizabeth's "most renowned stocke" who is also a *Steward* in Bess's household (italics mine).[4] This complicated picture of herself, so often taken by

---

[3]   This term is taken from Wall (2002, p. 5). Other accounts of the early modern household are provided by Korda (2002); Harris (1982); and Ezell (1987, pp. 37–8). For a discussion of the brutality that found a congenial setting in the early modern household, see Dolan, who explains: "While the household was an arena in which women were subordinate, it was also the arena in which they could most readily and legitimately exercise authority" (p. 210).

[4]   These descriptions are taken from Letter 6 and Letter 4 (addressed to Queen Elizabeth) and from Letter 1 (to her grandmother, Elizabeth Talbot, The Countess of

her contemporaries as well as by later readers as evidence of Stuart's derangement or of her cunning,[5] not only pervades the letters but structures them, I propose. This is because Stuart's letters, like the subject they describe, are also material things produced by the same "domestic routines" Guy describes, designed to be employed by others, as useful and as open to exchange, then, as any other household item. Stuart is not so much unsettling aristocratic claims but staking them forcefully at home (rather than at court), where imported items and exotic fineries took their place alongside homemade objects. Like any other household item, Stuart's existence is also based on the transmission of favors and services, as the letters repeatedly explain. Stuart's dependence on her grandmother for goods like affection, reading materials, a handful of trustworthy servants, even the barest rudiments of society, supports her many demands for autonomy in the same way that the bogus love affair she concocts in later interviews illustrates what she takes to be a sovereign claim. Such self-fashioning seems counterproductive, unless we also acknowledge the way Elizabeth's "Souverain[e]" power is likewise defined by Stuart as the ability to recognize the claims of one's kin, and thus to manage, without "commaud[ing]," a household much like the one a young Scottish queen could establish in faraway France, replete with routines and amusements, special clothing and loyal attendants. Subjects and objects were not opposed in the early modern household, but part of a continuum of duties and favors, debts and rewards that structured aristocratic households in nearly the same way that middle-class ones were fashioned.[6] Arbella's bid for freedom, or at least release from Bess's care, requires that she present herself as simply a more valuable object in Elizabeth's estimation, while reminding her Queen, too, of Elizabeth's own place within the household.

***

Like many wealthy widows, Bess was a landlord, moneylender, and merchant. And, like her queen, Bess presided over a sumptuous (and, from the 1590s on, husbandless) household. But Hardwick Hall hardly rivaled one of Elizabeth's courts. Richly appointed but located in remote Derbyshire, it was nearly a week's journey from London, and it lacked the games and fun that Mary Stuart had enjoyed with her four Maries, as well as the instruction the more studious Arbella would so greatly desire. Under house arrest for almost ten years, Arbella describes herself as both a basic part of Bess's household and an "exile" within, cut off from "Schollers, Musick, hunting, hauking," or "variety of any lawfull disport," as well

---

Shrewsbury). (See Steen, *Letters*, pp. 126, 122, 126, 119).

[5] Lewalski treats the contradictions (and resulting confusion) as limited to Stuart, rather than shared by all of Elizabeth's petitioners (pp. 72–5).

[6] See Stuart, Letter 16 (to Sir Henry Brounker) (Steen, *Letters*, p. 160). A useful account of the hierarchies operating within the early modern household is provided by Harris (1982, p. 143); Ezell (1987) explores the enormous power the wife wielded in the household (pp. 37–8). See also Hammons (2006) for a discussion of the fluidity of subjects and objects in the early modern period (1398).

as from the chance to attend her queen or be matched at court with a suitable husband.[7] Estranged from the life and position for which she had been carefully groomed by Bess after her parents' early deaths, Arbella gradually comes in her letters to see the household as a dangerous setting, a locus for spying, misprision, alienation, and treason.

Bess's guardianship of Arbella Stuart overlapped with the later years of Mary Stuart's captivity. No doubt proximity to the Scottish queen helped shape the child's image of the home, however expensive or "mundane" its comforts, as a kind of jail cell. In later years, Bess's commission for the renovation of Hardwick Hall (along with other ancestral properties) constituted an extraordinary challenge to the layout and purposes of the aristocratic household, notable for the increased access now provided to the lord—or in this case, mistress—of the manor,[8] and the lavish settings such houses might provide for political dynasties powerful enough to challenge sovereign rule. Indeed, opening up the household space by placing the great hall at the center of a symmetrical plan, and including vast corridors lined with glass and filled with light, Bess seemed to strive in her final years to avoid ever again being charged with the mean task of royal jailer.

Arbella Stuart's birth in 1575 appeared at first to herald another revision of sovereign ambitions. As the only child of Bess's daughter Elizabeth Cavendish and Mary Stuart's brother-in-law Charles Darnley, the fifth Earl of Lennox, Stuart's lineage put her front and center at a short list of heirs to Queen Elizabeth: certainly as Elizabeth's cousin and a native-born claimant, Arbella Stuart was a more attractive contender to some members of Parliament than was another cousin, Mary's son James VI. Even English Catholics found in her a reason to be optimistic, although Stuart never professed anything other than Protestant beliefs.[9]

Such dynastic hopes were early and repeatedly dashed, however. As a princess of the blood, Stuart was entitled to the Lennox lands and jewels provided by her father's line, but she never received them, collecting instead only a relatively small pension from the crown.[10] And she and Bess visited Elizabeth at court on just a few occasions—enough times for the queen to employ Arbella Stuart as marriage bait for the Spaniards—although nothing ever came of these machinations. In the very same way, Elizabeth had exploited her own marital prospects to maximum political advantage, but Stuart, in contrast, had no political position or finances to fall back on, and as anxieties about the succession mounted, the aging Elizabeth

---

[7] See Stuart, Letter 6 to Queen Elizabeth, and Letter 8 to Sir John Stanhope and Sir Robert Cecil (Steen, *Letters*, pp. 124, 135).

[8] For details see Friedman (1992). Miller refers to Friedman in her discussion of Bess's building projects (pp. 139–42). See also Levey (1998).

[9] Gristwood discusses some of the weaknesses of Stuart's position and, referring to a 1601 document prepared by Cecil's staff, reports that Stuart clearly stood second to James (pp. 136–48; 168).

[10] Lewalski offers details about Stuart's meager finances and weak familial network (p. 71).

Strange Bedfellows

made fewer overtures to Stuart, who was at one point lavishly praised by Elizabeth's lords for her learning, dancing, and writing.[11] We do not know whether the gifted Stuart somehow displeased her queen in the winter of 1592, or whether the longstanding rumors of a Catholic plot to kidnap Stuart had started to swirl again, but at this point, Elizabeth sends the teenager back to Hardwick Hall and to her grandmother's strict care, never to recall her again.[12]

What exactly happened at Elizabeth's court is difficult to answer, but how Stuart's prospects for personal or political success, once so dazzling, could nearly evaporate altogether is another question, suggesting that aristocratic families were also constructs underwritten by the state, with a generously endowed set of images and ambitions—in-laws and outlaws, too. The letters that the twenty-seven-year-old Stuart writes ten years later thus present manifold problems for critics, because they draw upon on an altogether different assortment of images, effects, and genres to tell the story of Stuart's fall and rise. These letters are unreliable and imperial, the stuff of romance and realpolitik, combining social-climbing fantasy and Oedipal desire with the formal requirements of a courtly petition.[13] (The image reproduced on the cover of this book of a two-year-old Arbella holding a doll–perhaps originally intended for Queen Elizabeth's tailor—depicts a similar fantasy, royal subjects and objects curiously reversed.) As desperate attempts to intervene in the business of the home and the state, we need to read them as pieces of an autobiography and as outrageous lies, confessional fragments and well-wrought fictions. Written in different hands—the formal secretary utilized for official business and the more informal italic reserved for personal (and typically female) exchanges—they provide evidence both of the extreme care devoted to household affairs and of the "accident[s]," as Stuart puts it, that could plague the household on a nearly daily basis.[14]

***

On the surface, what emerges out of Stuart's disappointed hopes on Christmas day in 1602 is a brazen scheme to arouse the ailing Elizabeth's worst fears: to have her think Stuart is planning to marry another royal claimant, the sixteen-year-old Edward Seymour, head up an army of Catholic supporters, and steal the throne. But these fears are baseless, as Stuart's subsequent letters to Robert Cecil, his agent Henry Brounker, her grandmother, and even the queen reveal; Stuart's plot,

---

[11] See Steen's introduction to Stuart's *Letters* for additional details about Stuart's marital prospects (pp. 19–20).

[12] Explanations for Arbella's exile from court are proposed by Gristwood (pp. 132–4); Lewalski (p. 70); and Steen (*Letters*, 1994), who cites rumors that Stuart was politically or personally involved with Essex (p. 21).

[13] For a discussion of aristocratic Englishwomen's "private" letters as social activity and political intervention, see Daybell (2004) and, in the same volume, Steen (2004, p. 155).

[14] Letter 6 to Elizabeth (Steen, *Letters*, p. 124). See Wilcox's (2007) discussion of the ways that different forms of early modern handwriting can also bespeak different goals, circumstances, or simply stages of thought (p. 18).

innocuous if not completely innocent, was instead designed to persuade Elizabeth to take a more solicitous view of Stuart's harsh plight, and to release her from Bess's keeping. Unfortunately, after the letters are confiscated, security around Stuart is further tightened, and she is more or less "marooned" at Hardwick, permitted no visitors, walks or riding, unchecked letters, or conversation (Lovell p. 408).

Yet the resulting transformation of Bess's household into a royal jail once more is only an extreme form of the charged loyalties and dependencies—sometimes rival ones—that characterized early modern households more broadly. At once a school, inn, factory, sickroom, nursery, and kitchen, this setting–no matter how grand or richly appointed–was probably noisy, smelly, and continually crowded with travelers, servants, close and distant kin, and retainers; neighbors and laborers had access, too, and material goods of all kinds were produced there, traded, consumed, and sometimes transported outside. Such a busy realm was organized and torn apart by different sets of rules: "competing allegiances" to work and to kin invited all kinds of strange bedfellows—stepchildren and cousins, laborers, and visitors. With ideas about authority, alliance, connection, and debt constantly in flux in this setting, "the domesticated subject," Wall (2002) argues, "was not simply passively molded within a fixed hierarchy, but submitted as well to uncomfortable modes of disciplining that set up multiple and discrete lines of dependency."[15]

If Arbella chafed under such "modes" of "discipline," she learned she could also manipulate them. Stuart's subversive letters were a product of such discipline and dependency, too; perhaps they were even written under the watchful eyes of her grandmother. As David N. Durant suggests, her bed had been moved into Bess's bedchamber after the Seymour episode (Durant, p. 207; see also Steen, *Letters*, 27). The extensive inventories Bess had prepared in 1601, cataloguing the vast contents of three households, shed little light on how such extensive letter writing might take place with such an estranged bedfellow in attendance. Indeed, the items Bess records are numerous, lavish, and costly, and in "Arbells Chamber" are listed "six peeces of hanginges of yellowe, blewe and otyer Couloured damask and sattin wrought with golde flowers and trees and lyned with Canvas, a bedsted, a mattriss, a downe bed, a wooll quilt[,]" along with a "Joyned stoole, a fier shovell, [and] a payre of tonges."[16] Stuart's few possessions seem rather meager for an adult woman, even an unmarried one (especially one of such "renowned stocke"), and it is also puzzling that they are counted among Bess's belongings in an inventory that lists six coffers for money in Bess's bedroom, too. Equally unusual is the way everyday needs and lavish desires compete with each other in this cramped space, the tools of a servant recorded alongside the comforts of a princess of the blood.

***

---

[15]   See Wall (2002, p. 3.)

[16]   These inventories have been collected by Levey (2001, pp. 54–5).

Yet Stuart imagines Elizabeth's court as similarly cramped, her letters suggesting that restrictions like the ones that governed Mary Stuart's imprisonment (or early life in France) characterized the lives of all noblewomen, and that women's domestic skills—like Mary Stuart's letter-writing and embroidery—were forms of statecraft dangerous enough to occasionally warrant an execution. Indeed, Stuart's letters of 1602–1603 provide a privileged glimpse of the workings of the aristocratic household as well as of its unusually close ties to Elizabeth's court, the ongoing succession crisis, even to the recent Essex scandal. In Letter 16, written in March 1603 on the second anniversary of Essex's execution and addressed to Cecil's agent Brounker, Stuart requests her Majesty's help in dealing with the anger of Stuart's eighty-year-old grandmother, describing the court as subject to the same strains and sentiments that could trouble the home. As Queen and cousin, Elizabeth is both part of and separate from these tensions, according to Stuart, and Stuart even argues that Elizabeth (herself nearing seventy years of age) is a victim of the same hard domestic discipline and manipulation: "Royall inclination would take with those of hir owne bloud, if it weare not <to my great astonishment> diverted from them, to those 2. counsellers kinred. They favour theyr kinred against hir Majesties, . . . doth hir Majesty favour the Lady Catherines husband more than the Earle of Essex frend? Are the Stanhopes and Cecilles able to hinder or diminish the <good> reputation of a Stuart hir Majesty being judge [?]" (Steen, *Letters*, p. 159).

Not only does Stuart here discount the political machinations of the Queen's two counselors in contrast to the needs of Elizabeth's "kinred," but political demands are clearly likened to those needs, the counselors' energies merely deployed in the service of a rival household, this one crudely staffed by men (the Cecilles, Stanhopes, and Lady Catherines husband). Ironically, Stuart reminds Elizabeth of a kin tie by minimizing the claims of domestic space.

If the familiar language of kinship could supply a set (or sets) of moral imperatives, in Letter 16 we also see how this language outlines an array of economic axioms governing the exchange and consumption of material goods, whereby favors might be "divert[ed]," pathways for exchange or the normal flow of "inclination" shut down, and "<good> reputations," as a result, "hinder[ed]" or "diminish[ed]."[17] Stuart's letters continually stake out these pathways and trade routes, not with the goal of being recognized as Elizabeth's successor but, instead, as a dependent in her household or in Bess's. Clearly Stuart is not a struggling woman writer, but a woman struggling for material security, since the goal behind the circulation of these letters is to continue their circulation—to preserve and extend kin ties, rather than leave this otherwise closed world and its endless demands behind. Accordingly, Stuart recognizes the "sovereignty" held by an "honoured, loved, and trusted kinswoman" rather than the sovereignty of her queen because Stuart's ambition is to be a recipient of good wishes, not a dispenser of them.

---

[17]   Harris (1982) explores some of the moral and economic precepts organizing the household (p. 146).

78 *Women's Wealth and Women's Writing in Early Modern England*

This presumption is not as self-defeating as it sounds; perhaps Stuart clearly recognizes something anthropologists will later theorize—and something queens might easily forget—that "persons are an artifact of the way in which relationships are handled through the possession and manipulation of things" (Strathern is quoted by Kuehn, p. 74). Stuart's self-worth (along with her material value as bride or princess) appears consistently tied to the effectiveness of her kin ties, for instance, and she is merely emphasizing her status as a household object, something which Bess's mistreatment or Elizabeth's paranoia was denying her. What is subversive, then, is not Stuart's repeated depiction of herself as a valuable thing, but her insistence that she really belongs to Elizabeth. With similar logic, she had reminded the Earl of Hertford in Letter 3 that he possessed "testimonies" which "[his family] and none but they have," credentials that might be used to appease (or mislead) her grandmother (Steen, *Letters*, p. 121). Interestingly, such "testimony," available in "any picture" or piece of "handwriting" produced by the Earl's female kin, primarily "testifies" to the Seymours' familial reputation and the strength of their connections: letters which challenge Tudor sovereignty, in other words, also substantiate family feeling and assume some of the considerable economic and symbolic power of the household, what Wall (2002) calls a "powerful fantasy of dependency" (p. 12) that rivaled the attractions and rewards of court.[18] Stuart's private aims as described in her letters—which were shared publicly at court and transcribed by Cecil himself—simultaneously challenge her queen's power by drawing on a cousin's love.

***

Letters were particularly useful instruments of state and of family life, as Karen Newman (1996) explores, nearly identifying the two centers of writing. In a "polity constituted along kinship rather than bureaucratic lines," Newman argues that social relations regularly took the form of gift-exchange, and in letters "[a]ll sorts of persons, men and women, young and old, high and low" were "objects negotiable and grammatical . . . procured, sent, commoned, presented, taken, had," and "made into things that [could] be handed out or assigned, struggled over and won" (pp. 142, 145). Along the same lines, Lynne Magnusson (2004) describes the importance of letters in a courtly world marked by scarce rewards and meager but costly favors. Forms of "social action and interaction," Magnusson even likens letters to "housework" "designed to carry out [the] rituals of maintenance and repair" constantly required by the crushing demands of politeness and politics (p. 52; see also Magnusson, 1999, p. 13). No wonder that Alan Steward and Heather Wolfe describe the letter as "the single most important genre of the Renaissance,"

---

[18] See Crawford (2006 B), who argues, "While much new historicist work, through its focus on state power, and, in particular, on the crown's own rhetoric of royal absolutism suggests otherwise, early modern England was not in practice an absolutist monarchy." Especially for many women writers, Crawford elaborates, "the royalism central to their literary activities was one in which power was diversified, subject to mediation and criticism, and located in multiple sites" (para 15).

Strange Bedfellows

"a period in which the culture of letterwriting," as they point out, "underwent several massive transformations" when print and the marketplace transformed readers into consumers (p. 10). Frank Whigham similarly describes how letters made use of "repeated rituals of affiliation" especially necessary in the intimate world of Elizabeth's court, one easily threatened by inattention or bad wishes, jealousy, a secret tie, or the rival affections of the king of Scots (p. 866; see also Clarke, p. 211).

Stuart's letters draw on and extend this expansive and demanding language of kinship, reworking personal despair as a challenge to the family, and reading in the family's "inheritance structures" a guide for nation-building, social codes and private ethics, even the shape of one's conscience or one's autobiography.[19] At the same time, emanating from within the household, indeed, produced by one of its most damaging secrets, the story Stuart records is a piece of domestic literature that has much in common with women's receipt books and prayer collections–copied, scribbled over, collaboratively produced and jointly decoded–and thus very different from the letters painstakingly modeled by Angel Day in the 1586 *English Secretarie*. Women's writings mostly circulate within households rather than between them.[20] "[B]oth set beyond the household and implicated within it," Stuart's letters—like her aunt Mary Stuart's embroidery—aim at release as well as at recovery, an escape from the household along with the means, this time sanctioned by the crown, to finally and securely return there.

Perhaps maidservants occupied a similarly ambiguous position in the aristocratic household; Bess as widow and magnate posed other problems to the integrity and order of this realm, too.[21] And the extent to which Elizabeth's power could challenge or penetrate Bess's carefully managed household was not always clear, either. Stuart exploits the uncertainty. In suggesting that she is a "product of many hands," Stuart creates confusion, for instance, over whether kin ties should be seen as "textual effects" (see Newman, 1996, p. 149) or more substantial things, byways or goals, sources or guarantors of meaning. This ambiguity is illustrated in Stuart's Letter 6, addressed to Elizabeth:

> [Y]our Majesty whose displeasure and not any punishment whatsoever is the onely thinge I feare and the feare of God makes me most secure and confident that I shall not onely avoide but that for ever winne or rather confirme that most evident and natifue affection which your Majesty hath ever from my cradle shown unto me above all other of your Highnesse most Royall linage . . . I resolved to crave my Grandmothers leave to present <my service> my selfe

---

[19] For a study of the way Anne Clifford's writings regularly experiment with different models of affiliation, thereby recasting private affections and courtly duties, see Crawford (2006 A, p. 1685).

[20] Additional details about how to read such "domestic work" are supplied by Field (p. 51).

[21] See Philippy's account of Isabella Whitney's ambiguous role in the household (p. 448).

80 Women's Wealth and Women's Writing in Early Modern England

unto your Majesty and if [that] I could not obtaine that (for even that small and ordinary liberty I despaired to obtaine of hir otherwise my most kinde and [gratiou] naturall parent) I determined that should be the first and I protest last disobedience that I would willingly offend her with. (Steen, *Letters*, p. 125)

Stuart details a primal scene replete with original preferment and a "first" disobedience, and even Elizabeth's "natifue affection" is forced into this Edenic image of childish debt and despair, made subject to that of someone who is "otherwise" a "kinde and [gratiou] naturall parent." Stuart's loyalties and transgressions are shifted between God and her Queen while blessings are imagined as things to "winne," as well as items in an inventory to "rather confirme." There is a strict calculus behind familial affection, and weighing Elizabeth's "displeasure" against "the feare of God," Stuart determines finally that her grandmother must be offended, a decision formed as much out of "protest" as, she notes, of "will." Just as revealing is the way that Stuart's "selfe" can be exchanged for her "service" in the letter. If these grammatical ambiguities map out some of the psychological and political fault-lines organizing and disrupting aristocratic affections and courtly obligations, they appear to complicate early modern piety, too.

With Elizabeth so boldly represented as a mechanism (in place ever since Stuart was in her "cradle") through which Stuart might appease her grandmother, it thus remains unclear whether the final arbiter of Stuart's plight (or "naturall parent" "otherwise") is Bess or Elizabeth, and whether the real reward would be love or liberty, political power or the chance, enunciated in Letter 16, to "be [her] owne woman"? (Steen, *Letters*, p. 168). Perhaps we do not need to answer these questions; more important, I think, is observing how difficult it is to disentangle them from each other. No wonder that the confusions extend to linguistic ones, given their origins in infancy, and Stuart explains the problem as involving both subjection and authority, telling Brounker in the same letter, "my meaning . . . is not my meaning" (Steen, *Letters*, p. 175).

Among the powerful "shaping fantasies" organizing the early modern imaginary were, Wendy Wall (2002) claims, fantasies of dependency—wishes to belong or be recognized, to have one's origins legitimized or affiliations feel powerful, to realize all of the rewards associated with being a child in the care of loving parents (p. 12). Such solicitude and indebtedness must have long typified the closeness Bess and her previous charge Mary Stuart had known. Addressed to her grandmother but designed for her queen's reading, Stuart's Letter 7 is another example of this fantasy of presumption and reward, where she grandly admits, "I am too stout to request a favour till I be sure I may command it" (Steen, *Letters*, p. 128). Perhaps such admissions of entitlement and indebtedness were heard culture-wide. The early modern family provided a framework for subjection through which favors might be regularly demanded or debts endlessly owed: Shakespeare's Hermione illustrates the family's wide reach and paternalistic power as a way to protect herself from her husband's cruelty, ironically protesting that she is subject

Strange Bedfellows 81

to another authority no less rigorous, paternalistic or forbidding when she tells Leontes the "Emperor of Russia was my father" (3.2).

***

That such a powerful imaginary also sets the stage for later havens or prisons is something Stuart makes clear in her many letters to Cecil or to Brounker, who was commissioned by the Queen to interview Stuart and determine whether her plans for escape or marriage were real and dangerous enough to be punishable. To these readers in particular, Stuart converts the political crisis she has sparked surrounding the succession, the handling of sedition, even the threat of treason, into a domestic dispute or family squabble—a wrangling of kin. But Stuart also figures this family battle as almost completely centered upon the writing and receipt and reading of letters, with their proper expression, interpretation, and circulation at issue. Like so many other goods that circulated in the household, the provenance and ownership of her story is constantly changing, too, troubled by many of the problems that plagued the production and circulation of early modern goods, including early modern women's writings, as Jennifer Summit (2000) claims. Summit argues that such writings "continually [raise] the question of what it means to create texts without the assurance of a permanent, unifying tradition, subject to the vagaries of transmission over which the writer has little control" (p. 29).

We see this question raised by Stuart in Letter 4, addressed to the Queen, where she begs from Elizabeth some formal reply or return letter "to signify your Majesties most gratious remission to me by your Highnesse letter to my Lady my Grandmother whose discomfort I shall be till then"—some proof, in other words, that the usual mechanisms for exchange remain in place, so that Elizabeth's forgiveness might inspire Bess's (Steen, *Letters*, p. 122). Another example is found in Stuart's instructions to her messenger, cited in my introduction to this book, where she requests the Earl of Hertford to provide "somm picture or handwriting" of the Lady Jane Grey (his dead sister-in-law, tried and executed decades earlier), in order that Bess might properly grasp or "confirm" Stuart's revisions to her own story.[22] That kinship should be interpreted as a story that could be subject to rewriting is suggested in Letter 7, where Stuart implores her grandmother to "give us all leave to impart our joy of hir Majesties pardon to us all one to another, and devise the best manner how to represent to hir Majesty the joy we conceive thearof and make ourselves marry with makeing our selves perfect in our partes" (Steen, *Letters*, p. 133). Not only will family members "make" themselves "perfect" by assuming their "partes," but this collaboration will be rewarded and advanced by the attendance of the queen.

Such reliance upon the circulation of stories obviously puts a check on any single individual's claims or influence, and there is little suggestion in Stuart's letters that Bess herself is a fount of favors or especially crucial source of affection, or that Stuart even sees Elizabeth in this way. Similarly, when James enters the

---

[22]   Letter 3. Instructions given to John Dodderidge for Edward Seymour, Earl of Hertford (Steen, *Letters*, p. 121).

82   *Women's Wealth and Women's Writing in Early Modern England*

scene in later letters, it is always as a cousin or lover, not as a patriarch. There are no mothers or fathers in Stuart's nursery, and nothing really loving in the bounty Stuart claims is owed to her.[23] As a princess in the household of her stepmother, Elizabeth had long ago analyzed the same impersonal if efficient workings of the household and its limited magic in a July 1544 letter to Katherine Parr:

> Inimical Fortune, envious of all good, she who revolves things human, has deprived [me] for a whole year of your most illustrious presence, and still not being content with that, has robbed me once again of the same good: the which would be intolerable to me if I did not think to enjoy it soon.[24]

The princess does not beseech Parr's affection but a thieving Fortune's cooperation because the tie between the two women is envisioned as something that can also be robbed or postponed, a "good" subject to loss or an object to be promised—nothing to be taken personally. The tie with Henry, recently renewed thanks to Parr's labors, was construed along the same limits. In a letter to her father written that same year, Elizabeth prefaces another gift, a translation of Parr's prayers, with the following wish: "May I, by this means, be indebted to you not as an imitator of your virtues but indeed as an inheritor of them," implying that the evidence of textual influence can actually establish royal paternity and desert better than any shared feelings or blood.[25]

The proposition that texts can produce or reproduce biological effects is repeated in Stuart's letters, and she explains in Letter 16 that she has suitors, secrets, and enough "poeticall fictions" to support her royal designs, allowing her to exchange her "mourning weede" for a "gorgeous change of . . . suite" (Steen, *Letters*, p. 174). Rumors, lies, and gossip are represented, in contrast, as poorly crafted goods or gifts that fail to keep alive the cycle of exchange, and Brounker is told about the "secret whisprings" of Stuart's detractors,

> shaping it as best pleaseth theyr fancy <who> have made you present hir Majesty with a mishapen discouloured peece of stuffe fitting none nor fitt for hir Majesty to looke upon which if either I might be suffered or not hindred I will not say helped but why should I not be helpet I pray you in such a peece of worke?

Stuart represents herself here through her suit and as one, and even the solution to her harsh situation is strictly a material one. Stuart argues that she

> [s]hould have binne presented to hir Majesty in a forme well beseeming hir Majesty wheras now it is so tossed up and downe that it hath almost lost the

---

[23]   Kahn explores the courtly world of favors and debts under James I (pp. 36–7).

[24]   Elizabeth I, *Collected Works* (p. 5.)

[25]   Ibid. p. 10.

Strange Bedfellows 83

glosse, and even by the best slubbred up in such hast that many wrong stitches of unkindnesse must be picked out which need not have been so bestowed and many wrong placed conceits ript out. (Steen, *Letters*, p. 166).

Nowhere does Stuart propose any other metaphor for herself than that of a household object, even if that object is something jointly produced, with "many wrong placed conceits." When she later pictures herself as autonomous and authoritative, she preserves this imagery, announcing: "I must take it hand, and shape my owne cote according to my cloth," adding, "but it shall not be after the fashion of this world god willing but fit for me" (Steen, *Letters*, p. 166).

***

Writing was not always central to the affairs of early modern women who wrote. But women who wrote wanted to produce something that was more than an effort or shadow of their circumstances—a valuable object in a household crammed with many other things that women would want to own or share or copy. If we are troubled (or disappointed) by the way early modern women's writings, even Stuart's unusual productions, seem to rely upon or spring out of the cares and accidents of the household—in contrast to more canonical literary works prized for their form or craft, their freedoms or what Virginia Woolf calls their "incandescence" (p. 57)—we overlook the fact that early modern women were not permitted this opportunity, nor really interested in it. Few early modern men were interested in such "incandescence" either, I suspect. Instead, to have their writings be of their worlds was a signal achievement, and that so many writings of early modern women are "all grown about with weeds and bound with briars," as Woolf puts it (p. 61), turns out to be a rich metaphor, the weeds and briars emblematic of the vital networks so powerfully bringing women together.[26] That Arbella's letters function at once as confessions, legal documents, and romance fictions illustrates their success as well, signifying their reach into a wider network of courtly advisors, relatives, and other readers eager for such fare.

Even her outrageous overture to the Earl of Hertford on Christmas Day 1602 makes sense in this way. On the one hand, Stuart is exploiting any means of escape, but the Seymours had their own legitimate claim to Elizabeth's throne, and a union between Arbella Stuart and Edward Seymour would be a most advantageous match. The Seymours of course had a prior history as usurpers in their own right, the Earl (son of the Lord Protector and brother of the *Hecatodistichon*'s three authors) imprisoned by Elizabeth after a clandestine marriage to Catherine Grey (sister of the executed Jane Grey); both of the sons from this union (one of them the father of Stuart's proposed husband) were declared illegitimate by the crown.[27]

---

[26] See Woolf's description of the "hostile" environment and instincts crippling the woman writer's efforts (pp. 56, 61); and Ezell's comments on Woolf's "myth" of Judith Shakespeare (1993, pp. 39–65).

[27] For additional details about the scandal and its aftermath, particularly during the years of Arbella's courtly troubles, see Breight.

84   *Women's Wealth and Women's Writing in Early Modern England*

As I briefly explored in Chapter 1, the queen had long ago been involved with Thomas Seymour when she was in the care of her stepmother Katherine Parr, whom Seymour married in 1547. In proposing a marriage with Hertford's grandson, Arbella Stuart is therefore aligning herself with a family of sexual and political intriguers whose proposals and progeny were always grasped by the crown as utterly subversive, the personal here political, dangerous, and unlawful.

Stuart's other fantastically subversive conceit of the home is provided by the image of the king of Scots as Stuart's secret co-conspirator and tutor, her lover's identity only revealed to Bess after Elizabeth's curiosity had been aroused by the first six letters. Yet drawing James into her story has the effect of proving Stuart's loyalty and demonstrating family feeling, too, since Stuart's preferring James over the Seymours in later letters means returning to the world of her immediate kin. "Embracing the absolute" or getting into bed with patriarchy offers a way for Stuart to make herself Elizabeth's equal as well (see Gallagher), and in Letter 6 to Elizabeth, Stuart offers James as a bribe or gift that will thereby reconnect them:

> I shall thinck my selfe most happy if hir Majesty will grace him with hir favor and winne his heart from me if it be possible, and I will dayly pray for hir Majesty and him that he may dayly deserve hir Majesties favour more and more as I know he will indeavor. (Steen, *Letters*, p. 132)

Stuart's letters offer Elizabeth a version of their family romance that renders mothers and fathers sisters and brothers, erases national borders, and converts Bess's ancestral property into a home roomy enough for all of Elizabeth's subjects to "grace" and "favor" and "winne" each other.

***

Perhaps the "problem" of the woman writer in early modern England has less to do with the fact of her writing and more with the lack of a ready-made audience for her work—or with some failure in the writer's relations with other women (see Ezell, 1993, p. 43). Even male critics often attacked early modern women writers on these grounds: Lady Mary Wroth was enjoined not to silence by Lord Denny, but to align herself more closely with the efforts of her aunt Mary Sidney Herbert, a translator of psalms and author of closet drama. Doubts about sufficient family feeling were sometimes expressed by women writers themselves: Elizabeth Clinton, the Countess of Lincoln, was more disturbed by her failure to nurse any of her 18 children, for instance, than by her impulse to record this regret in a 1622 treatise on breastfeeding. What is so striking about Arbella Stuart's writings is the way they aim to educate her audience about how to read women authors, explaining over and over again how to best weigh their kinship claims.[28] Edith Snook helps us understand such a strangely twinned project, arguing that

---

[28]   See Snook, who explores how women writers "insist that reading is socially important, within a private devotional practice, within the family, in relationships between women, as well as between women and men, and within the state" (p. 24).

"[r]eading, the act of interpreting, mediating, and personalising texts, cannot be, and in early modern England, was not, separated from the structures of hierarchy and authority" (p. 58).

Yet perhaps what Sara Jayne Steen (1998) describes as Stuart's "self-fashioning" in her letters must also take into account that this is a self created with remarkable craft and incredible abandon and the knowledge that its expressions can be decoded and intercepted, copied or filed away—and thereby rendered material, over and over again. Stuart shapes a fiction of possession and deserving that can tolerate distortion, withstand relentless interrogation, and exploit the pervasive sense that its author is a liar (see Steen, 1998). Such an "artifact," to use Marilyn Strathern's terminology, is on display even in the courtly papers Brounker helps Stuart assemble after his interrogation, where recorded is Stuart's guilty plea, qualified in every possible way:

> I protest my conscience doth not accuse me of any fault hearin but a small, honest necessary and consequently most pardonable presumption for which I doubt not but to obtaine pardon in regard of the satisfaction and expiation I offer to make thearfore which I know will be acceptable to hir Majesty and weare sufficient pennance for the greatest offence as I take this is the smallest that ever was made. (Steen, *Letters*, p. 148)

Stuart makes herself disappear from her confession and then reappear as queen in this new, improved version of her autobiography, recreating herself as both lover and beloved, parent and child, ruler and ruled. One way or another, Elizabeth loses power in this economy of corrupted texts, but it is no wonder that the Queen was so wary and finally so sympathetic to Stuart. Could one imagine a more ungrateful—or a more devoted—daughter?

The tradition of women writers and readers which Stuart outlines in her initial instructions for Hertford—a tradition which includes Lady Jane Gray, Gray's sister Catherine, and Queene Jane Seimer—envisions queens and sisters and mothers as authors, readers and models, with a valuable inventory of texts all in need of Elizabeth's "gratious interpretation" (see Steen, *Letters*, pp. 121, 124). Such an audience never takes place, however. Instead, the Queen dies in March 1603 and Stuart is released from Bess's custody a month later, joining James's court in July 1603. Like his predecessor, however, the king of Scots refuses Arbella her lands or the chance to marry; and when the thirty-five-year-old Stuart contracts a secret marriage with the twenty-two-year-old William Seymour (Edward's younger brother) in 1611, the newlyweds are permitted only a brief happiness before the two are separately imprisoned. Bride and groom each escape (Stuart disguised as a man, with rapier and doublet) before Stuart can be transferred further north, probably to Scotland, but she is quickly apprehended and locked in the Tower, where she dies at age 40, rumored to be insane and, from her trusted doctor's accounts, in tremendous physical pain.[29]

James and Elizabeth's anxieties about Stuart do not appear entirely unfounded, given Stuart's repeated plotting, extensive letter-writing, and frequent attempts at escape. Indeed, Stuart's letters painstakingly shape a rival world—not unlike the universe Mary Stuart embroidered in her long captivity—out of the raw materials of family feeling, royal paranoia, and the syntax of goods and favors which welded court and home together. Her sovereign creations presage those queens which many later women writers will imagine holding court after the death of Elizabeth—figures like Elizabeth Cary's Mariam, Lady Mary Wroth's Pamphilia, or Margaret Cavendish's "Margaret the First," all of whom enjoy their considerable powers to love or to write or to be their own women in private, their households completely empty or broken apart. If we finally see Mary Stuart's life as, in contrast, curiously humble, both its beginning and end confined by the routine pleasures and cares of the household, Arbella Stuart's efforts transform the household into a powerful, even dangerous place of desire and ambition. At the same time, it is a place where Elizabeth herself might feel comfortable and beloved: "hir Majesty onely excepted" in Stuart's vision, as she maintains in Letter 7 to Bess, "parents, kinne, and the world" "already forsaken" (Steen, *Letters*, p. 132). Even if we view Arbella Stuart's short and difficult life as marked, biographer Sarah Gristwood claims, by a "series of mistakes" (p. 429), the story Stuart circulates in her letters supplies an utterly different picture, neither of triumph nor of tragedy, but of imperial power all the same.

---

[29]   In her introduction to Stuart's letters, Steen (1994) quotes extensively from the official statements of Stuart's personal physician, Dr. Thomas Moundford (pp. 85–6).

Chapter 5
"Girles Aflote"

I know you huswifery intend, though I to writing fall.

I lost two cities, lovely ones. And, vaster,
some realms I owned, two rivers, a continent.
I miss them, but it wasn't a disaster.[1]

In the final years of a very long life, Elizabeth Talbot, Countess of Shrewsbury, spent lavishly to inscribe herself on the exterior walls of Hardwick Hall, the grand manor home she had commissioned from architect Robert Smythson. On each of six turrets Bess had writ large the letters "ES," her initials resting atop a massive building of alabaster, sandstone, and glass (all materials gathered from Bess's many properties), such that other residents of remote Derbyshire—or any visitor from court—would see the writing and be suitably astonished, even from several miles away.[2] There are other early modern women who strive to place their writings amidst similarly large and luxurious settings, and they take almost the same great pains to extol their surroundings—whether imposing country homes or crowded cityscapes—in clearly loving detail, inventorying the rich contents of houses or stores, counting out these place's inhabitants and their various stations, and recording, with both precision and understanding, the complicated rules governing the circulation of favors and goods within. It is rare, though, to include Bess of Hardwick among them—either as a writer or as a property-holder—or, indeed, to recognize any of these early modern women as part of a larger accounting project or poetics of possession, perhaps because their representations of material abundance and wealth are frequently estranging ones, just as often marked by isolation, loss, or alienation. This is the case with Bess's imposing initials, too, the signs of a widow who is moneyed and landed, but also obviously remote from us.

Just as rarely do we put the writings of two other early modern women together, rough contemporaries of Bess, although the poetry of Isabella Whitney and Aemilia Lanyer similarly outlines worlds of abundance in which they have learned to write

---

[1]   The epigraphs come from two sources; the first, from Isabella Whitney, 'To Her Sister Mistress Anne Baron,' rpt. In Martin 287; the second, from Elizabeth Bishop, "One Art."

[2]   Radically different overviews of the construction of Hardwick Hall are offered by Friedman (1992) and Durant: Friedman sees Bess in terms of her powerful status as widow and builder; Durant's reading of Hardwick Hall, in contrast, emphasizes Bess's outsized ambitions and extravagant spending (pp. 157–63, pp. 179–82) . See also Lovell, Hall (p. 8), and Frye (2000), who provides another context for women's letters.

Fig. 5.1   New Hall at Hardwick

and to think, places where reading takes its place alongside the crucial activities of buying and selling, giving and trading. Women's biographies tend to be driven by the raw materials of emotion and biology, even when the stories women share and wants they describe privilege economic matters and emphasize patrons rather than family, clothing rather than love. Such material concerns are often at the center of many early modern women's writings, however, something we see rather starkly when we put Lanyer's 1611 country-house poem "The Description of Cooke-ham" (which predates Ben Jonson's 1616 "Penshurst") next to the imagery of urban life supplied by Whitney's 1573 *Wyll and Testament*, which one set of editors characterizes as "a shopper's guide to Elizabethan London."[3] The two worlds these poems describe are not as opposed as one might think: the state of nature on view at Cooke-ham is achieved through the intervention of tremendous skill and aristocratic grace (the raw rather expertly Cooke[d]), while the damage inflicted by Whitney's London is as severe as the harm bred by any other harsh climate, its population ravaged by famine, disease, and waste.

Yet each poem also uncovers entirely different systems of reward and need, drawing on disparate measures of authority and relation. In her *Wyll*, Whitney (c.1540–after 1580) imagines herself at once as cast-off servant and dejected suitor, neglected by and odds with a cruel and indifferent urban world which routinely seems to punish women, for "many Women foolyshly," Whitney's speaker explains, "Do such a fyxed fancy set, / on those which least desarve" (lines 7–10).[4] Still, the metaphors of crushing power and unrequited desire in Whitney's *Wyll* are outnumbered by the images of an urban machinery that so perfectly divides people from each other, for London not only deprives the speaker of credit, but also refuses to "releve" her with "Apparell" (lines 21, 23), and puts other women's "Plate and Jewells" in danger of being "mard with rust" for lack of use (lines 248–9). The ties that once held families firmly together have been completely severed, and London's streets are here represented as home to "Maydens poore," "Roysters," "Ruffians," and "Girles aflote" (lines 240, 136, 142, 243).

There is irony, of course, in that Whitney's *Wyll* proposes to bequeath to readers objects which do not belong to her, just as Lanyer's poem celebrates the riches and beauties of a household now permanently shut down; but there is another irony in the fact that Lanyer, almost 40 years later, is lamenting the decline of women's favors and goods in a world apparently already lost to Whitney, many years before. No wonder that instead of the luxuries and comforts of the now-forsaken Cooke-ham, Whitney provides two other commanding settings for unhoused women, a hospital and poorhouse, respectively named Bedlam and Bridewel (lines 263, 268). Unlike Whitney, who probably did spend at least her early years as a maidservant,[5] Lanyer (1569–1645) was more closely connected by birth and through marriage (to royal musicians) to the courts of Elizabeth and James, and thus had been a guest of sorts at Cooke-ham, the estate presided over by Margaret, Countess of Cumberland and her daughter Anne Clifford (who will wage and eventually win a war against male family members to retain her familial property). Yet this haven for women is also mapped out hierarchically: through a top-down distribution of rewards and favors itself mandated by lineage and history, mothers advance

---

[3]   See the editors' notes on Isabella Whitney in *Early Modern Women Poets: An Anthology* (p. 48).

[4]   This and all references to Whitney's "Wyll and Testament" are taken from the edition prepared by Clarke (2000) and will be noted parenthetically in the text.

[5]   Ellinghausen offers a rich discussion of Whitney's material circumstances and the choices they permitted her as a woman and as a writer; see also Travitsky (1980); and Wall (1991).

daughters, patrons sponsor authors, and nobles generously inspire their inferiors. All of this Lanyer registers with nostalgia and gratitude, her Eden denoted by the unimpeded transmission of original gifts, "where . . . first obtain'd, / Grace from that Grace where perfit Grace remain'd" (lines 1–2).[6] Even in detailing the countess's departure from Cooke-ham, Lanyer's contrast is not with the debilitating poverty and misery which Whitney's London begets, but with the joys of heaven. There is no other human habitation that can compete with Cooke-ham, in other words, because there the "dimme shadowes of celestiall pleasures" are found, pleasures "[w]hich are desir'd above all earthly treasures" (lines 15–16).

Despite these vastly different pictures of wealth and community, Whitney and Lanyer both turn to writing to explore and even calculate their losses and expectations, their expenditures and debts.[7] How, though, might we assess Bess's writings alongside those of Whitney or Lanyer? Does the fact that Bess builds a country house instead of writing a poem about one make her letters any less influential or instructive? Or does the magnitude of Bess's accomplishment—like a giant sampler still standing four hundred years later—require another set of critical tools, like the ones we have devised to read women's writings that were nearly lost (and continue sometimes to seem unimportant), works that appear at one with other household chores or resemble other pieces of household stuff—like Princess Elizabeth's New Year's gifts or Mary Stuart's needlework—and thus are "scarcely visible as literature [,] even now"?[8] In this case, it is almost as if the size (and repetition) of Bess's initials makes us think less of her as a writer—or as if her great wealth precludes her need of an inventory.

Yet we might group many early modern women's works together, I think, as small—or sometimes immense—efforts to manage their wealth. Throughout this book, I have proposed that we read early modern women's writings as collaborative, social, and, above all, as material objects primarily concerned with the circulation of other material things. Such a perspective compels us, Margaret J.M. Ezell maintains, to focus on women's "modes of production" rather than upon the patriarchal "means of repress[ing]" women who write and thereby to study the writings of housewives along with the writings on houses, mother's advice books next to lyric poems—and to uncover a tradition out of what was shared and copies rather than from what was thought or felt.[9]

---

[6]   This and all references to Lanyer's "The Description of Cooke-ham" will be taken from the edition prepared by Clarke (2000) and noted parenthetically in the text.

[7]   Hammons (2005) and (2006) supplies a useful set of economic readings of early modern women's poetry.

[8]   Fleming offers a rich starting point for this kind of handling of women's work in her review of Lewalski. See also Ezell (2002).

[9]   See Ezell (1993, p. 43). Miller (1998) explores these questions in terms of the authority early modern women assume as writers, commenting on Lanyer's choice "to write not a prose polemical pamphlet or a mother's advice book . . . but a long sequence of lyric poems" (p. 148).

Fig. 5.2   One of Bess's letters, from a set of six initials that adorn the top of New Hall at Hardwick

***

It is with such a picture of women's reading and writing in mind that Carol L. Winkelmann analyzes "what literacy meant for women in the seventeenth century," exploring whether erudition or eloquence, for instance, counted as highly as moral applicability or family feeling, and whether families might draw on female literacy—along with other modes of sustaining kinship—in ways that other social relationships did or could not.[10] Sometimes kinship cannot be sustained, anyway. Chapter 4 explored the manifold uses to which Arbella Stuart puts her letters, but one might wonder what she is doing in 1610 when she decides to sell to her godmother Mary Talbot some of the needlework panels that her grandmother, dead two years, had produced in collaboration with Mary Stuart 40 years earlier—aside from raising enough capital to finance another escape.[11] Arbella Stuart's unusual transaction reminds us of the bequests in Whitney's *Wyll*, where giving things of value now means giving them away: in trading an heirloom for hard cash, Arbella may also be signaling a disruption in the world of women that had long surrounded her. Perhaps irrelevant, possibly bankrupt, this early modern network

---

[10]   Winkelmann argues that "despite an inhospitable climate for women's writing, women participated in significant literacy events" (p. 14).

[11]   Accounts of this transaction are supplied by Gristwood (pp. 368, 475–6); and Steen (*Letters*, p. 160).

of women and the goods and favors they readily traded in apparently had less to offer women like Arbella, who was, by then, closely connected to James's court but also orphaned, unmarried, and deprived of a birthright of lands and jewels. The widowed Lanyer and unemployed servant Whitney offer useful parallels to the single woman Arbella's situation, their accounts recording losses both material and personal, and their definition of wealth always linked to things that women might circulate.[12]

If Arbella opts to forego this women's world in selling the panels to one of Bess of Hardwick's daughters, choosing money over the wealth that women might share, most single women of the time had little choice in the matter, left to themselves in their teens with few friends or relations, especially if economic hardships brought them to London to seek out work as maids (see Jones, 1999, p. 21). The poverty and mistreatment maids frequently endured could be short-lived or long-standing; if they remained alone or found themselves unemployed, the absence of female kin must have been especially difficult to bear. Amy Froide portrays their situation as a dire and yet invisible one because, while "[w]idowhood had a public and independent place within the patriarchal society[,] singlewomen did not" (p. 237).

Women's networks were, however, also shrinking at this time, at least partly because many women like Arbella increasingly found themselves—especially those among the peerage and the poor—"not married . . .[being] either widowed . . . or never married."[13] This demographic fact has economic as well as literary implications, shaping both the structure of society and the way it might reproduce itself. Up until the early seventeenth century, networks of female kin had not only been extensive but powerful in both rural areas and the city: indeed, in the uppermost reaches of society, these networks carried substantial political weight and social influence. Barbara J. Harris (2002) explores, for instance, how courtly mothers and wives only a generation before had used their influence with Tudor monarchs to negotiate marriages, arrange places for their children, even monitor the disposition of lands or revenues.

Sometimes, Harris notes, early modern women's favors were restricted to other women; but at other times, husbands or sons or other male kin could benefit. For instance, there were advantages for many women in the coterie universe described by scholars like Jane Donawerth and Margaret Ezell, a literary world characterized by dense ties of readers and writers who traded manuscripts among themselves.

---

[12] Lanyer even imagines courtly benevolence in terms of female favor; in a dedicatory epistle to *Salve Deus Rex Judaeorum*, she states that "great Elizaes favour blest my youth." See Mueller (1994) for a discussion of Lanyer's "feminist poetics" (p. 209). Bennett and Froide supply details about the economic and social circumstances of single women in early modern England.

[13] For demographic statistics, see Erickson (1993, p. 9); Lanser provides additional details about the political controversy surrounding and economic hardships facing single women (p. 306).

Intimate circles of women writers might rival networks of male authors for output and ambition, but sometimes they included male readers and writers. In any case, early modern literary culture, as Ezell emphasizes, was social. Money, therefore, counted as less of a reward than esteem, affection, or reciprocity.

Ideas about gender need to acknowledge the economic ways that influence and power are culturally defined: as economies change, the constraints or possibilities of gender are altered as well, and the resources a mother provides—like inordinate love, her treasured needlework, or the confidence of two queens—can seem priceless to one set of heirs, almost worthless to another. Forgetting this, we tend to think of female influence as always indirect and intermittent, easily distracted, not something that extends beyond the family, survives the household, or shapes culture at large: women might transmit things here and there, but not authority in the long run. As Thomas Kuehn usefully puts it, "[t]here was no unity and continuity or succession to women as there was to men," and he cites the work of Yan Thomas, who likewise argues that early women "were deprived of institutional extensions of their singular personhood" (p. 64). But there were other ways for early modern women to extend their reach, however, other ways their influence might survive their deaths. These include, Pamela Hammons (2006) notes, the means through which women "deployed legal instruments, such as wills and settlements, on behalf of themselves and other women to gain control of property" (1387). Other writings—like women's letters or poems—exhibit additional ways of pooling resources or managing relationships.

Much of the time, though, early modern women corroborated the patriarchal framework of things, rarely challenging the way property was distributed, stories written, children educated, or houses maintained.[14] Indeed, Arbella's own sorry fate, so many years a captive in her grandmother's house, is a good illustration of the way dynastic matters might be entirely and reliably governed by women at home.[15] But the conclusions we draw should not fault or minimize early modern women's labors. Working with legal documents drawn up to assist in the dispensation of the property of Florentine women, Kuehn urges us to consider another model of female agency or personhood that is unrelated to modern notions of "individual freedom and self-determination" (p. 59). Florentine women (and many Florentine men, he notes) routinely acted in concert with their families, their desires or goals inseparable from those of husbands or fathers or sons. Such collusion took place not only because patriarchal pressures were so oppressive, but because early modern men and women understood themselves mainly in terms

---

[14]   Along the same lines, Matchinske argues, "We need to remember that women writers of the early modern period did not often question dominant masculinist literary modes of production. They did not defy generic expectation. Nor did they altogether reject the assumptions on which those modes and expectations depended. To do so would have been untenable" (p. 435).

[15]   As Klein (2001) argues, "For the aristocratic wife, the role of mother is one where domestic and dynastic obligations intersect" (p. 21).

of relationships to others: an individual self might be useful at one moment, less crucial at another, and if the needs of kin were more urgent or apparent, they might also coincide with the particular wants of a parent or sibling. The family was thus a tremendous "arena for female agency" at this time, as Kuehn maintains, a site of influence and prestige, support and reward.

At first glance, the early modern form of "social personhood" Kuehn describes appears governed by subordination, accommodation, passivity. But the evidence he assembles instead characterizes a self mobilized by the project to actively, deliberately, and carefully help shape other selves. Early modern women's efforts were particularly organized by such reproductive goals, since mothers and stepmothers, sisters, aunts, and godmothers almost equally supplied time and talents to their kin. These networks also provided goods and favors in the course of building and maintaining a family's well-being and connections, and the items exchanged among women of all classes demonstrate both care and concern for this system of concerns. Queen Elizabeth's coronation robes and Mary Stuart's needlework, as explored in previous chapters, are such valuable pieces of property in this women's world precisely because they are so easily recycled, cloth especially attractive to symbols of the self and its ties to other selves.

All of these connections appear to be broken in Arbella's transaction with Mary Talbot, in service of something even more valuable, perhaps—Arbella's freedom or the marriage (with William Seymour) that 850 pounds could buy. Single women like Arbella often had an altogether different set of plans for themselves about where they would live, what they would do with their belongings, even what ideas they would share. Yet I think Bess's interior and exterior designs for Hardwick Hall similarly overturn the model of women's gift-exchange outlined thus far. Whitney might link the two of them together, ironically placing "wealthy Widdowes" (line 206) below the "Girles aflote" (line 205) in her *Wyll* as evidence of a world in which women's favors have lost their value. Single women like the "girles" and "widdowes" Whitney describes also challenge the ways a mother's power might be construed in the early modern period by calling into question whether she is ultimately the source or recipient, authority behind or interpreter of other women's works. Whether propertied or propertyless, single women might be both enriched and impoverished when they hoard their things, refusing to trade them with other women or to turn them over to a responsible patriarch.[16]

***

Complications surrounding women's property have continued to trouble our sense of what mothering does or means; even Virginia Woolf conjures up a foremother in Shakespeare's sister, only to imagine Judith Shakespeare poor and childless.[17] And until very recently, Bess of Hardwick's story was the stuff

---

[16] See Korda's (2004) account of the cultural anxieties "associated with the figure of the propertyless and the propertied singlewoman" (p. 137).

[17] Rich describes the legacy of this confusion as also a literary one, arguing that "the cathexis between mother and daughter is the great unwritten story," "little evidence"

"Girles Aflote" 95

of legend and insult too, the few times it was told. But early modern women's networks have a rich history, politics, set of valuables, and laws of exchange to which we have not always attended. Official documents are lacking, and the players themselves were often taught not to care. Yet the social and political worth of these ties—and of the material things which substantiated those connections— could be enormous. The New Year's gifts regularly bestowed on Queen Elizabeth during the period between Christmas and Twelfth Night, for example, offer a first-hand guide to the stature and influence of courtly women's networks. Gifts to the queen were carefully recorded by Elizabeth's advisors, and rolls of donors in turn scrutinized by the Queen.[18] As Jane Donawerth reports, male nobles, clergy, and senior officials more often gave purses of gold than goods like books or cloth or jewels; on the other hand, the women surrounding Elizabeth, including servants, members of her Privy Chamber, and the wives of nobles, frequently gave material things, including, in 1584, a "cusshyn, handkercher, a bodkyn of golde, two canes of ivery," and "brusshes the handels enbrodered" (see also Nevinson, 1975, pp. 28–9). Other gifts in other years, Janet Arnold (1988) reports, included slippers, loose gowns and petticoats, ruffs and smocks, hose and socks. Elizabeth summarily reciprocated in the afternoons with "carefully graded gifts of silver-gilt plate," a return of considerably less value than the bulk of the gifts she had received in the morning (pp. 93–4). But more important to the donors were the grants of favors, titles, and liveries from the queen that might follow in the year to come. The women in her inner circle might also expect cast-off clothes, jewels, and places for their children.[19]

If the outlay of funds and labor was not as high, there were still other exchanges and expenses that preoccupied early modern women from nearly all classes throughout the year in a constant circulation of jewels, plate, advice, recipes, prayers, and children, even (as we saw in Chapter 2) the "trauncelating" of a female relative's gowns and kirtles. Increasingly, however, this early modern women's world was undermined as a variety of imported goods, including expensive linens, carpets, spices, and other "needeful knackes" nicely catalogued by Whitney's *Wyll* (line 66) flooded the market, such that the poet's authority now is strikingly tied to her bestowal of things she neither owns nor ever could afford. What happens when the material objects long circulated by women were compared to these new

---

of which exists "in theology, art, sociology, even psychoanalysis" (pp. 225–6). See also Hirsch; and Ruddick, who explores the philosophical and political costs of ignoring the story or the tie it describes.

[18] Durant discusses some of Bess's gifts to her Queen (pp. 91–2). See also Nevinson (1975); Arnold (1988, pp. 95–6, 177–81); Klein (1997); and Donawerth.

[19] See Arnold (1988) for other details about many of these gifts, including their materials, donors, and makers. A study of the women who made up Elizabeth's inner circle is provided by Somerset (pp. 60–93). Jane Lawson's study of Elizabeth's New Year's gift rolls is forthcoming.

96   *Women's Wealth and Women's Writing in Early Modern England*

fineries? And what happens to women's networks when material things—designed to accumulate rather than circulate—became precious in themselves?

Behind these questions, I think, is a larger one about what happens when women ignore or refuse the assumptions, pathways, and relations that had longed guided daughters' lives—when women decide, in other words, not to mother each other. Many of Bess's vast holdings, for instance, were explicitly withheld from exchange, meant to be displayed as symbols of her wealth and ancestry, not exchanged in service of a wider circle of kin; with age and wealth, her inventories continue to record additional purchases and furnishings, even as the list of grandchildren and extended family grew ever longer. Some children—like her firstborn, Henry—or grandchildren—like the wayward Arbella—even found themselves disinherited, and accounts of Arbella's later life at James's court repeatedly refer to her huge gambling debts and extravagant spending on clothing and jewels; the Venetian ambassador's 1607 report describes Arbella as "[w]ithout mate and without estate" (see Lovell, p. 463; and Newman, 1989, pp. 513–15). These reports present Arbella as a casualty of a world that was being eclipsed, even though, ironically, Arbella was now living the life for which Bess had so carefully groomed her, "given the sought-after role of Trainbearer to the Queen, and . . . treated with the greatest honour and deference." "Indeed, thanks to her grandmother," Mary Lovell observes, Arbella "was perfectly suited to just this role" (pp. 452–3). So Arbella's sale of something that previously would have been exchanged among women tells us much about the changing nature of female influence and relation in the early modern period, while her economic difficulties provide evidence of the poverty and abjection many single women felt in a world increasingly less animated by gifts, more centered around consumer goods.

***

Maureen Quilligan suggests that such estrangement and depletion—or the emptying out of maternal legacies—provides conditions out of which a tradition of women's writing can emerge. Early women's writings, Quilligan argues, halt "the traffic in women," since a woman's sharing of ideas almost necessarily meant resisting marriage and the rule of the patriarch, in the process also privileging one's natal origins (like Anne Clifford's at Cooke-ham) or endogamous ties (like Mary Wroth's incestuous relationship with her cousin).[20] In addition, women's literary authority often takes its shape from—and centers its stories upon—refusals to mother. Naomi Miller rightly comments in her reading of "The Description of

---

[20]   Quilligan (2005) cites the work of Weiner and Mauss in her study, which proposes that Renaissance culture "imagines female agency as a monstrous growth predicated on incestuous female desire" (p. 5). Elsewhere, Quilligan claims that female agency empowers and is empowered by an "endogamous assertion of family prestige" (p. 27), and she takes up Bess of Hardwick's life and accomplishments briefly in this discussion, to comment that "Elizabeth Talbot exercised her agency by bringing back to her native place the status and wealth she had acquired through marriage: even though she had been 'trafficked' away in these marriages, she was able still to keep close to her natal origin" (p. 184).

"Girles Aflote" 97

Cooke-ham" that Aemila Lanyer describes others in the poem as mothers, but noteworthy, too, I think, is the exception the poet herself provides, always a child or beneficiary in this now-depleted, abandoned realm.[21] Being estranged, unemployed, unmarried or disinherited becomes something like an enabling condition, then, as the amazing career of Arbella's grandmother also attests, because even aristocratic women who enjoyed the prestige and security afforded by tremendous wealth and connections might explore other ways to claim power or articulate relation once they were widowed. Puzzling out Bess's place in this changing world of women can help us better grasp the kind of authority and influence early modern women writers might likewise hope to achieve. Looking at the records and purchases Bess carefully left behind in account books and inventories spanning more than thirty years provides us, for example, with portals into the nature and transmission of wealth as well as its gendered and social origins. It supplies us too with a fuller sense of the variety of material forms that women's writings could take and the manifold ways that their influence could be transmitted (see Ezell, 2007, p. 34). Married four times, with six surviving children (from her second marriage to Sir William Cavendish), Bess had moved from the ranks of minor gentry into the upper level of Tudor aristocracy. She serves as a striking model of the vagaries as well as the vicissitudes of female authority, the uncertain hold it frequently had over its belongings (in this case, scattered across 20 miles of lands), its pose of sufficiency and affection, and its dense, nuanced vocabulary of objects, expenses, textures, lengths, colors, and trim.

If there is little evidence of the matriarch's power or holdings in any of Shakespeare's plays, many early modern authors nonetheless shared Bess's material concerns, and their writings busy themselves with descriptions of objects and the authority these objects substantiate, Lear's robes and Othello's mother's handkerchief only the most obvious examples. Dympna Callaghan reminds us to look more deeply at such material things: Shakespeare's Othello is "uncannily preoccupied," for instance, "with artifacts wrought by female hands, both esthetically prized and mundane" (pp. 55–6). Perhaps the very range of female abilities and products—from hand-sewn sheets to hand-copied poems, descriptions of Cooke-ham or blueprints for an ancestral home at Hardwick—produced anxiety or confusion, too, over who should get to own or use these valuables, and what they might mean as a result.

Being an early modern daughter or mother comes with a cache of goods, expenses, and obligations, as we can see by attending to the objects Bess carefully assembles throughout her long career as wife, mother, moneylender, landowner, merchant, and, in her final years, mistress of three houses with over two hundred rooms to furnish. In so doing, we will also apprehend how the circulation or alteration of objects creates a history, such that the "trauncelating" of a sister's gown or cutting up of a tapestry is at once a political fact, sociological event,

---

[21]   Cf. Miller (1998), who writes: "My concern [is] with Lanyer's strategic constructions of women as (m)others to each other" (p. 146).

98   *Women's Wealth and Women's Writing in Early Modern England*

and psychological process (see Hammons, 2006, p. 1398). At the same time, we can distinguish between "competing ideas of property" at work in Bess's long career, differences sometimes originating in the separate demands of being a wife, mother, and estate manager.[22]

A maid-servant to wealthier relations, Bess is widowed for the first time at the age of 16. She was widowed three more times, with each loss amassing more property, until she became, with the death of George Talbot, Earl of Shrewsbury, the richest woman in England, save for the queen. She shows up regularly on the New Year's Gift rolls, but she was also—as James Daybell observes—a frequent recipient of gifts and information herself, energetically sought after by many courtiers because of her wealth, her influence with the Queen, and her reputation for business sense and political savvy.[23] The many letters addressed to Bess by female kin housed at the Folger Shakespeare Library (Folger MS X. d. 428) similarly underscore her enormous influence and authority. The language these letters draw on is rarely affectionate, always deferential, and yet we can also detect in them a subtle transformation of women's debts and relations as Bess's status and inventory improves.

Early letters from contemporaries treat the delicate pushes and pulls operating behind the exchange of New Year's gifts to Elizabeth. An October 1568 letter from Elizabeth Wingfield, a member of Elizabeth's inner circle and Bess's half-sister, relays that the queen has a "good opennon of [Bess]" after Bess's gift of venison to Elizabeth, so much so that the queen had confided, "there ys no lady yn thys land that I beter love and lyke." Little wonder that Wingfield shrewdly closes her letter to Bess with a pledge of continued service to her addressee, "your honors to command" (X.d. 428: 129). Another letter from Wingfield, written January 1576–1577, reports on the success of Bess's New Year's gift: "[H]er ma[jestie] never liked any thinge you gave her so well the color and strange triminge of the garments." The royal reward is immediate, if insubstantial, for Wingfield says a grateful queen now "geve[s] out suche good speeches of my lordship and you[r] la[dyship] as I never hard of better" (X. d. 428:130). That gifts—often handmade—were more valued than cash would be noted years later in a December 1585 letter from Wingfield, reporting that she and Lady Cobham, another member of the circle of ladies surrounding the queen, had "longe confarde of the matter" and "she was muche against your la[dyship] giving money" (X. d. 428: 131). Bess's two friends instead forward directives for a gown for the queen.

Women assume their social identities as wives and mothers in the course of shaping other women, physically, socially, morally, and I would add, economically, the physical closeness prompted by childbirth and childcare quickly subsumed by more abstract requirements of household management, schooling, religion, and marriage.

---

[22]   For an investigation of some of these different understandings of property, see Chan and Wright (p. 163).

[23]   See Daybell (2004, pp. 117–18) and, in the same volume, Steen (2004) for a related treatment of Bess's kin networks and the power they wielded at court.

Daughters and sisters are produced in the course of meeting demands that also involve the use or exchange of material goods, and such exchanges also motivate many of the letters written to Bess over the years by daughters, female friends, and granddaughters. An early letter from Arbella Stuart dated 8 February 1587–1588 accompanies a gift from the twelve-year-old child: "[T]he ends of my heare which were cutt the sixt day of the moone" and a "pott of Gelly" (Steen, *Letters*, p. 119). Over and over, a sentimental language of love is repeatedly sidestepped by (or reinvented through) a rhetoric of debt, obligation, devotion, duty, and abasement. The connections are ongoing and extensive, with great returns of social capital and political yield; Bess is invariably "My dear Madam," her health (generally excellent) is always solicited, her gifts carefully, gratefully, and promptly recorded. The effect over the years is to create the picture of a financial wizard, real estate tycoon, and trusted ally of the queen, someone seemingly short on advice or affection, but well endowed with taste, resources, and cash. We see this in a 1575 letter from Bess's eldest daughter Frances Pierrepont that accompanies New Year's gifts of "a peece of Lawne and a drinckinge glasse" sent in "lyke desire of your blesinge unto Mr. Pierrepont and me and our children." Frances's letter aims, in fact, to continue this cycle "as a remembrance" of my "lovynge dutie;" as she avers to her mother, "I am soe muche and many wayse bounde unto you as none can be more and so neare unto you as none can be near" (X. d. 428: 67). This letter was written a month or so after Frances's sister Elizabeth had given birth to Arbella, and some polite shoving over proximity to Bess might be expected, given the baby's birthright as a princess of the blood and potential successor to the queen.

Such a regular and carefully recorded transmission of gifts can seem cold to us, as if family ties were thin enough to require the evidence of goods and services. But Barbara Harris (1990) reminds us about the overwhelming influence of the inheritance system on the structure of the family and upon women's relationships within it: the battleground, Harris claims, "was therefore property," and controlling familial assets could reshape whatever biology had planned (pp. 630–31). The constant circulation of gifts and favors should also remind us that early modern motherhood lacked an official system for transferring wealth, maintaining order and degree, assigning influence, or controlling and consolidating power. Unlike fatherhood, which clearly aims to ensure patriarchy's transmission of objects and power, motherhood historically replicates itself through acts of depletion, its narratives worked out through tropes of poverty, sacrifice, and self-denial.

***

Few of these tropes apparently govern Bess's extensive efforts to accumulate and retain her property, however. Even her model status as a noble wife raises complications to our model of mothering: Bess and her fourth husband were so well regarded as loyal subjects by their queen that Elizabeth entrusted them with the care of Mary Stuart for 16 years; and less than 20 years later, Elizabeth would insist upon Bess's strict guardianship of Mary's niece Arbella. Yet every pledge of service served as way to accrue royal power for the Shrewsburys, too: Mary's custodians had to be extremely careful with their charge, for instance, just in case

Mary legally or illegally assumed Elizabeth's throne. Understandably, Bess and Mary became friends and even, rumors suggested, helpmeets, Bess sharing court gossip with the Scottish queen and possibly obtaining Mary's cooperation in arranging Elizabeth Cavendish's 1574 marriage to Charles Darnley. Household chores could serve as another means to redefine aristocratic authority or even sovereign power (as explored in Chapters 3 and 4). For one thing, much of the needlework jointly produced by Mary and Bess in the 1570s and 1580s ended up furnishing one of Bess's many properties; indeed, Arbella's sale of some embroidered panels to Mary Talbot might even be construed as putting back into circulation an object Bess had noticeably withheld from exchange.

There are other complications which Bess and her labors present to our picture of early modern women's wealth and influence. For 16 of the 23 years she was married to George Talbot, Bess's household space was really one of Elizabeth's jails, her properties (and those of her husband) an extension of the court, with an almost constant stream of royal visitors, spies, foreign ambassadors, and retinue of servants, priests, and hangers-on. We need thus to consider closely the accomplishments of this period with Stuart—which Francis de Zulueta strangely depicts as "long years of inactivity"—as domestic only by default (p. 5). Both of them more or less under house arrest, the two "spinsters" find a way to collaborate on the stories of their lives: along with the official impresas and coded messages that Mary embroiders onto cushions, wall hangings, and a series of panels, we find Bess stitching messages, emblems, and musings of her own about the twists and turns of her married life. Bess includes, for instance, a tribute to her second husband and father of her six children, William Cavendish, in a centerpiece of tears embroidered with the motto "Extinctam lachrimae Testantur Vivere flamman" (Tears witness that the quenched flame lives), the impresa, Margaret Swain (1973) notes, of Mary's mother-in-law Catherine de Medici (p. 75). A number of other Cavendish emblems also appear alongside the monograms of her fourth husband, suggesting that George Talbot's affections were only one of many favors Bess drew on to describe her destiny, and that widowhood only furthered—and did not initiate—Bess's story-telling.

So striking is the nature of the collaboration between the two women: if Mary's work is more allegorical and classical, Bess's work, sometimes described as inferior or pedestrian, seems to me just as driven by her own dynastic ambitions, her fourth husband's uneasy involvement notwithstanding.[24] Simply put, the two women share the same goals in these works. The wall hangings Bess would later purchase for Hardwick Hall are just as ambitious, just as personal. Depicting the Virtues—Zenobia with Magnanimity and Prudence, Artemisia with Constancy and Piety, Cleopatra with Fortitude and Justice, Lucretia with Chastity and Liberality, and Penelope with patience and Perseverance—these hangings all feature images

---

[24]   See Ellis's study of the hangings, although she, like Levey (1998, p. 58) and Swain (1973, pp. 63–4), seems to downplay Bess's contributions.

"Girles Aflote" 101

Fig. 5.3 One of Bess's needleworked panels, with her initials and the symbols of mourning for her second husband Sir William Cavendish

Fig. 5.4 The Cavendish hanging in full, which includes one of Mary Stuart's royal monograms

of wives and mothers as inherently and similarly regal.[25] When Santina M. Levey estimates the value of Hardwick's grand furnishings, she comments that the

---

[25] Cf. Ellis (p. 285). See also Frye (1999) and Quilligan (2005), who comment on the claims for both female agency and endogamy made by the "cloth-draped interior of Hardwick Hall," where the embroideries displayed there depict "militant female virtues– famous historical women, female allegorical virtues conquering tyrants" (p. 48).

huge collection of lavish and costly textiles in the form of pillow covers, carpets, bedcovers, and wall hangings "represented a capital investment greater than that of the house itself." Bess's fourth marriage foundered in part over quarrels about such investments, including linens that were eventually judged, Levey (1998) notes, too worn or spoiled even to be used (p. 15).

There were extensive architectural projects over which Bess presided, too, among them the restoration of Old Hall at Hardwick (for her second son, William, because Chatsworth was entailed on her oldest son, Henry) and the building of New Hall there, a project dramatically enlarged once Bess became dowager countess with Talbot's death in 1590. We should see these projects as analogous to Bess's needlework, since both are grandiose reconstructions of female space, genealogy, and wealth, her initials prominently embroidering both. And both projects also make use of others' labors to tell a commanding story of the self. As royal jailer and now, as architectural patron and supervisor of a "small army" of masons, sculptors, carpenters, and glaziers nearing, Lovell claims, 350 workers, Bess almost single-handedly rewrites whatever meaning any increasingly isolated household space was beginning to acquire in the period, by demonstrating how great power over things could inform or symbolize a power over people.[26]

Not only the expenditure but also the design of New Hall is significant. The entrance door opens directly into the great hall, altering the traditional access of visitors to the head of the household who was, in this case, a woman. Such direct visual and physical access to the great house, in addition, creates a new form and meaning for the country house, according to Alice T. Friedman (1992, pp. 41–3, 50–51). New Hall includes a gallery 162 feet long and 26 feet high, displaying four portraits of Bess. The overall effect is in tremendous contrast, Friedman (1992) notes, with more conventional images of women "as essentially recessive, nurturing, and domestic" (p. 43). Instead, New Hall expresses just how far a mother's powers might extend and the striking ways that they might rival those at court, by specifically emphasizing where quarters for favor or affection might reside, and also suggesting that such places have no walls, at least ones that cannot be looked through.

Hardwick is an impressive setting for Bess's wealth to reside and also to be kept out of circulation; Arbella comments on the transparency of this fortress when she describes Hardwick as crowded with "grave overseers" in a letter to Elizabeth's councilors (Steen, *Letters*, p. 134). As Santina Levey (2001) records, many household furnishings specified in Bess's will were to "remayne and Contynewe" in the houses (Levey, 2001, p. 22), managed by her son William but not given to him outright (pp. 9–10). These items describe a world of comfort and warmth, but there is little sense of the mental or social activity they might reflect or generate:

---

[26]   For details about the New Hall's laborers and expenses, see Lovell (pp. 350, 390). Friedman offers a rich description of the building project (1995).

104 Women's Wealth and Women's Writing in Early Modern England

> In the high gatehouse Chamber, a mattriss, a pallet case, an inlayde Chare [and] the same Chamber verie fayre waynscotted with Coloured woodes set out with portalls and some alabaster and other stone. In the Inner Chamber, a playne bedsted a fetherbed a mattriss a bolster a pillowe, three fledges a Coverlet, a playne forme, too joyned stooles, too quitions a payre of bellowes. (Levey, 2001, pp. 9–10)

Room after room and chamber after chamber are crowded with the same luxuries, goods that seem to merely pile up outside of history, freed from exchange, and unaltered by human use. This is very different from the world Isabella Whitney catalogs, replete with "foode" from Butchers, "juels" and "woollens," charged by the "desyres" of "quiet persons" and "Ruffians" alike (ll. 103–4). Whitney's world is one of poverty, infection, and quarrels, all "procu[ing] further care" (ll. 151–2), and thus requiring continuous exchange, something Bess's will has overruled.

***

Just as different from Bess's impulse to collect things is Arbella's decision to put one of her grandmother's objects up for sale: a work jointly produced by two of Arbella's forbears—with all of its dense imagery about the complications of their maternal lives—is rejected by its only real heir, the circle of in-laws rent apart by the outlaw Arbella. A changing relation between women and things is on display in Whitney's poetry, too, and she explores the repercussions of this change on the shape of property, the claims of the family, and the power of the affection that once seemed to organize life within the wealthy household. But this time, the household is viewed from the outside, by someone inventorying the London markets of luxury goods which increasingly found themselves imported into aristocratic households like Bess's. Whitney's estrangement from this world is as complete as it is impoverishing: as Danielle Clark notes, Whitney's "lament is not for a lost sexual relationship, but for the lack of social and material connection to the world."[27] In fact, Laurie Ellinghausen argues that Whitney's isolation "is at least as important as her allusions to past and present communities;" Ellinghausen suggests that as a "poor, single woman who explicitly claims to write for money," Whitney's "individual" agency is set in explicit contrast to the agency long provided women by the arena of the family, with none of the links to kin to protect it or inventory of goods to substantiate it. Indeed, the persona of a maidservant, Ellinghausen maintains, is a "means of expressing [Whitney's] tenuous relationship to her own literary property."[28] But I think the persona also supplies stark evidence of the failure of female community, circulation, and exchange.

The issue of control of material goods—so important to early modern mothers—is central to Whitney's identity as a writer, and she, therefore, supplies a striking founding figure for a female literary tradition in England, since she makes

---

[27] See Clarke's (2000) introduction (p. xvi).

[28] See Ellinghausen and Wall (1991). Additional background is provided by Travitsky (1980).

it abundantly clear she has no goods to leave her readers. Her poem questions both the premises and values of the older system, and the discrepancy she detects, introducing herself as "whole in body, and in minde, / but very weake in Purse" (lines 1–2), is refigured as the difference between a text circulating in the marketplace and one being read by a select group of readers. For that reason, perhaps, a new and greatly disembodied sense of power and obligation motivates the dedication of her miscellany *A Sweet Nosgay* to George Mainwaring, a benefactor. The poet admits she had hesitated in publishing the volume because "so little of my labour was in [the] verses that they were not . . . to be esteemed as recompence for the least of a great number of benefits." Yet Whitney overcomes her reluctance with the need to "shew my selfe satisfed, gratifye your Guifts" and "accquit your curtesies." Her language thus points in two directions, repaying and canceling, acknowledging a system of benefits while opting out of it, telling Mainwaring: "It is the giver: not the guift, thou oughtest to respect" ("The Auctor," line 50).

What instead gives substance to Whitney's avowed aim is the glut of goods available in London:

> In many places, Shops are full,
> I left you nothing scant.
> Yf they that keepe what I you leave,
> aske Mony: when they sell it:
> At Mint, there is such store, it is
> unpossible to tell it. (lines 107–12)

The wealth here is "Mony" that cannot be counted, material that outnumbers the favors and goods of kin and bankrupts any family history. Not only has the speaker lost her position as a maidservant, but the household has also been apparently emptied out, and Whitney's aim is, therefore, not to win security or affection, but to alleviate desire and exile need. No wonder she never mentions returning to home as a solution in the poem; "Such Goods and riches which she moste aboundantly hath left behind her" are all housed in London. In "One Art," written nearly four hundred years later, Elizabeth Bishop will mull over the same bankruptcy that characterizes the female poet's existence. Bishop outlines a cosmos where the speaker and her things are forever parting, and explains such losses as necessary training for the poet, since measuring things becomes equivalent to renouncing them: "So many things seem filled with the intent / to be lost / that their loss is no disaster."

But early modern women teach us that there are other ways to calculate wealth or underwrite disaster. If the world of female kin was being actively stripped away by some women, its belongings sold off, its comforts found thin, its dominion— even at a vast place like New Hall at Hardwick—rendered small and isolated, the financial diary of spinster Joyce Jefferies for the years 1638–1649 suggests a different picture of a single woman's independence and influence, because she invests in agricultural projects, loans money to male kin, and regularly patronizes

106 *Women's Wealth and Women's Writing in Early Modern England*

local female merchants and craftswomen.[29] The image of regal Penelope, presiding over a world of strangers and suitors and repeated, Margaret Ellis notes, throughout many of the furnishings of Bess's estates, is another such figure, whose endless household labors are really just a cover for her own secret desires, and who derives authority from what she refuses to need.[30]

***

The language of lost property also animates the captive Arbella's letters explored in Chapter 4, her stranded figure offering another example of a female world more and more shaped by dislocation or disinheritance, poverty, and debt. Early modern women's inventories of failed ambitions or broken connections take their place in what Michelle M. Dowd and Julie A. Eckerle call an "increasingly textual world" (p. 1), even as reproduction became even more immediately defining and circumscribing of women's activities, according to Nancy Chodorow (pp. 12–13), and the household reordered as a special site of female labor and female poverty. Hardwick Hall would not only be something like a contradiction in this new universe, but an uninhabitable one at that. Still, if single women found themselves increasingly cut off from motherhood's transformed role and obligations, they sometimes discovered themselves freed from the restrictions this new identity imposed. Arbella's letters dramatize this change in the world and highlight women's awkward place within it. They also exploit the range of political and social opportunities this change offers, once Arbella is forced to operate outside of the family and transact business by deliberately cutting up its fabric.[31] Alongside what Lawrence Lipking calls the "obstinate image" of the abandoned woman haunting poetry and discarded by her lover (p. 1), we might thus place the equally authoritative images of the unmarried daughter who renounces things and the widowed mother who hoards them.

The literary tradition stretching all the way from Aphra Behn to Sylvia Plath would seem to house such single women nicely, women whose writings have much in common with the labors of Shakespeare's cast-off spinster Bianca, whose earnings as a seamstress and copyist need to be supplemented by prostitution. Such "spinsters" seem cut off from each other; they also are often childless, "aflote," or employed in someone else's home. But they have significant economic power as producers and consumers, and they remind us that there are many kinds of legacies that women can leave behind, whatever authority they possess. Actually, such legacies are sometimes the only means through which early modern women's authority can be said to exist, in creating relation, describing a tie, enforcing a debt. Women writers rarely fail in these worlds, for there are many ways to leave one's name behind or to reproduce the letters that make up the story of oneself.

---

[29] See Ostovich and Sauer (pp. 265–71).

[30] Donawerth comments on "the unifying concept of the exchange of gifts" in *A Sweet Nosgay* without referring to the grinding poverty Whitney also details (pp. 14–16).

[31] See Daybell's (2004) discussion of the broader social and political consequences of this transformation in his introduction (p. 17).

Virginia Woolf suggested that the dearth of women writers in Shakespeare's day was linked to the poverty of their mothers; indeed, that "women have always been poor, not for two hundred years merely, but from the beginning of time" (p. 108). We now know better, however, seeing that nearly all early modern women had things of value to share, exchange, or finally bequeath to their daughters and sisters. Even if most of these women did not write or did not produce works "visible to us now" as literature, they, nonetheless, helped to shape what Margaret Ezell (2002) calls "the literary culture" of the time, creating material things that forged connections, described ties, and assumed important meanings and relationships (p. 121). When such a women's world collapses, as Amelia Lanyer suggests in "The Description of Cooke-ham," their poetry is temporarily silenced. "Faire Philomela leaves her mournefull Ditty," Lanyer's speaker laments, "Drownd in dead sleepe, yet can procure no pitttie"(lines 189–90).[32] Yet in another poem, this one addressed "To the Lady Arabella," Lanyer implies such a loss is ultimately "no disaster." She describes Arbella Stuart—whom Whitney, years earlier, might have viewed as one of the "girles aflote" pictured in her *Wyll*—as instead one "well accompanied / With Pallas, and the muses." And this "Great learned lady," a "Rare phoenix," can fly: as Lanyer's speaker boldly reminds her reader, long stranded in one jail or another for so much of her short life, your "fair feathers are your own" (lines 10–11, 1–4).[33]

---

[32] See Hammons (2005), who maintains that "women's poetry of dwelling place is typically grounded in the loss or ruin of the physical site being represented" (p. 396).

[33] Aemila Lanyer, "To the Lady Arabella." Rpt. by Salzman (p. 28).

Bibliography

Ajmar, Marta. "Toys for Girls: Objects, Women and Memory in the Renaissance Household." In *Material Memories: Design and Evocation*, edited by Marius Kwint, Christopher Breward, and Jeremy Aynsle, pp. 75–89. London: Berg Publishers, 1999.

Arnold, Janet. "The 'Coronation Portrait' of Queen Elizabeth I." *Burlington Magazine* 120, no. 908 (1978): 727–30.

——. "Jane Lombard's Mantle." *Costume: The Journal of the Costume Society* 14 (1980): 56–72.

——. *Queen Elizabeth's Wardrobe Unlock'd*. Leeds: W.S. Maney and Son, 1988.

Ashelford, Janet. *Dress in the Age of Elizabeth*. New York: Holmes and Meier, 1988.

Batho, Gordon R. "A Prisoner's Pursuits: The Captivity of Mary, Queen of Scots." *The Historian* 12 (1986): 3–8.

Beal, Peter, and Margaret J.M. Ezell, eds. *Writings by Early Modern Women. English Manuscript Studies 1100–1700*. Vol. 9. London: The British Library, 2000.

Beilin, Elaine. *Redeeming Eve: Women Writers of the English Renaissance*. Princeton: Princeton University Press, 1990.

Bennett, Judith M., and Amy Froide, eds. *Singlewomen in the European Past, 1250–1800*. Philadelphia: University of Pennsylvania Press, 1999.

Bishop, Elizabeth. *One Art*. NY: Farrar Straus and Giroux, 1976.

Bowden, Caroline. "The Notebooks of Rachel Fane: Education for Authorship?" In *Early Modern Women's Manuscript Writing,* edited by Victoria E. Burke and Jonathan Gibson, pp. 157–80. Aldershot: Ashgate, 2004.

Breight, Curt. "*Realpolitik* and Elizabethan Ceremony: The Earl of Hertford's Entertainment of Elizabeth at Elvetham, 1591." *Renaissance Quarterly* 45, no.1 (1992): 20–48.

Brown, Elizabeth. "'Companion Me with My Mistress': Cleopatra, Elizabeth I, and Their Waiting Women." In *Maids and Mistresses*, edited by Susan Frye and Karen Robertson, 131–45. New York: Oxford University Press, 1999.

Brown, Georgia E. "Translation and the Definition of Sovereignty: The Case of Elizabeth Tudor" In *Travels and Translations in the Sixteenth Century. Selected Papers from the Second International Conference of the Tudor Symposium* (2000), edited by Mike Pincombe, pp. 88–103. Aldershot: Ashgate.

Brown, Sylvia, ed. *Women's Writing in Stuart England: The Mothers' Legacies of Dorothy Leigh, Elizabeth Joscelin, and Elizabeth Richardson*. Phoenix Mill: Sutton Publishing, 1999.

Burke, Mary. "A Question of Balance in the Sonnets of Mary, Queen of Scots." In *Women, Writing, and the Reproduction of Culture,* edited by Mary E. Burke, et al., pp. 101–18. Syracuse: Syracuse University Press, 2000.

Burke, Mary E., Jane Donawerth, Linda L. Dove, and Karen Nelson, eds. *Women, Writing, and the Reproduction of Culture in Tudor and Stuart Britain.* Syracuse: Syracuse University Press, 2000.

Burke, Victoria and Jonathan Gibson, eds. *Early Modern Women's Manuscript Writing: Selected Papers from the Trinity/Trent Colloquium.* Aldershot: Ashgate, 2004.

Callaghan, Dympna. "Looking Well to Linens: Women and Cultural Production in *Othello.*" In *Marxist Shakespeares,* edited by Jean Howard and Scott Cutler Shershow, pp. 53–81. NY: Routledge, 2000.

Carter, Alison J. "Mary Tudor's Wardrobe." *Costume: The Journal of the Costume Society* 11 (1977): 9–28.

Cavallo, Sandra. "What Did Women Transmit? Ownership and Control of Household Goods and Personal Effects in Early Modern Italy." In *Gender and Material Culture in Historical Perspective,* edited by Moira Donald and Linda Hurcombe, pp. 38–53. Basingstoke: Macmillan, 1999.

Cavanagh, Sheila." The Bad Seed: Princess Elizabeth and the Seymour Incident." In *Dissing Elizabeth: Negative Representations of Gloriana,* edited by Julia M. Walker, pp. 9–29. Durham: Duke University Press, 1998.

Chan, Mary, and Nancy E. Wright, "Marriage, Identity, and the Pursuit of Property in Seventeenth-Century England: The Cases of Anne Clifford and Elizabeth Wiseman." In *Women, Property, and the Letters of the Law,* edited by Nancy E. Wright, et al., pp. 162–82. Toronto: University of Toronto Press, 2004.

Chodorow, Nancy. *The Reproduction of Mothering: Psychoanalysis and the Sociology of Gender.* Berkeley: University of California Press, 1978.

Clark, Danielle, ed. *Renaissance Women Poets: Isabella Whitney, Mary Sidney and Aemila Lanyer.* NY: Penguin, 2000.

Clarke, Elizabeth. "Beyond Microhistory: The Use of Women's Manuscripts in a Widening Political Arena." In *Women and Politics,* edited by James Daybell, pp. 210–27.

Clinton, Elizabeth. *The Countesse of Lincolnes Nurserie* (London, 1622). Rpt. in Travitsky, *Mothers' Advice Books.* Aldershot: Ashgate, 2001.

Cole, Mary Hill. *The Portable Queen: Elizabeth I and the Politics of Ceremony.* Amherst: University of Massachusetts Press, 1999.

Crawford, Julie. "The Case of Lady Anne Clifford; or, Did Women Have a Mixed Monarchy?" *PMLA* 121, no. 5 (2006): 1682–9.

———."Women (Authors) on Top." *Early Modern Culture: An Electronic Seminar* 5 (2006). http://emc.eserver.org/1-5/crawford.html

Crawford, Patricia. "The Construction and Experience of Maternity in Seventeenth-century England." In *Women as Mothers in Pre-Industrial England,* edited by Valerie Fildes. New York: Routledge, 1990.

Bibliography

Daybell, James. "'Such newes as on the Quenes hye wayes we have mett': The News and Intelligence Networks of Elizabeth Talbot, Countess of Shrewsbury (c. 1527–1608)." In *Women and Politics in Early Modern England*, edited by James Daybell, pp. 114–31. Aldershot: Ashgate, 2004.

——, ed. *Women and Politics in Early Modern England, 1450-1700*. Aldershot: Ashgate, 2004.

de Grazia, Margreta. "The Ideology of Superfluous Things: *King Lear* as Period Piece." In *Subject and Object in Renaissance Culture*, edited by Margreta de Grazia, Maureen Quilligan, and Peter Stallybrass, pp. 17–42. NY: Cambridge University Press, 1996.

Demers, Patricia. "The Seymour Sisters: Elegizing Female Attachment." *Sixteenth Century Journal* 30, no.2 (1999): 343–65.

de Zulueta, Francis. *Embroideries by Mary Stuart and Elizabeth Talbot at Oxburgh Hall, Norfolk*. Oxford: Oxford University Press, 1923.

Digby, George Wingfield. *Elizabethan Embroidery*. London: Faber and Faber, 1964.

Dolan, Frances. "Household Chastisements: Gender, Authority, and 'Domestic Violence'." In *Renaissance Culture and the Everyday*, edited by Fumerton and Hunt, pp. 204–25. Philadelphia: University of Pennsylvania Press, 1999.

Donaldson, Gordon. *The First Trial of Mary, Queen of Scots*. Westport, CT: Greenwood Press, 1983.

Donawerth, Jane. "Women's Poetry and the Tudor-Stuart System of Gift Exchange." In *Women, Writing, and the Reproduction of Culture*, edited by Mary E. Burke, et al., 3–18. Syracuse: Syracuse University Press, 2000.

Dowd, Michelle M., and Julie A. Eckerle, eds. *Genre and Women's Life Writing in Early Modern England*. Aldershot: Ashgate, 2007.

Duffy, Eamon. *The Stripping of the Altars: Traditional Religion in England, c. 1400–1580*. New Haven: Yale University Press, 1992.

Durant, David N. *Bess of Hardwick: Portrait of an Elizabethan Dynast*. NY: Atheneum, 1978.

Durkan, John. "The Library of Mary, Queen of Scots." In *Mary Stewart*, edited by Michael Lynch, pp. 71–101. Oxford: Blackwell, 1988.

Elizabeth I. *The Miroir or Glasse of the Synneful Soul*. In *Elizabeth's Glass*, edited by Marc Shell. Lincoln: University of Nebraska Press, 1993.

——. *Collected Works*. Edited by Lean S. Marcus, Janel Mueller, and Mary Beth Rose. Chicago: University of Chicago Press, 2000.

Ellinghausen, Laurie. "Literary Property and the Single Woman in Isabella Whitney's *A Sweet Nosgay*." *SEL* 45 (2005): 1–22.

Ellis, Margaret. "The Hardwick Wall Hangings: An Unusual Collaboration in English Sixteenth-Century Embroidery." *Renaissance Studies* 10 (1996): 280–300.

Erickson, Amy Louise. *Women and Property in Early Modern England*. NY: Routledge, 1993.

Erickson, Carolly. *Bloody Mary: The Remarkable Life of Mary Tudor*. New York: Doubleday, 1978.

Ezell, Margaret J.M. *The Patriarch's Wife: Literary Evidence and the History of the Family*. Chapel Hill: University of North Carolina Press, 1987.

——. *Writing Women's Literary History*. Baltimore: Johns Hopkins University Press, 1993.

——."The Posthumous Publication of Women's Manuscripts and the History of Authorship." In *Women's Writing and the Circulation of Ideas: Manuscript Publication in England, 1550–1800*, edited by George L. Justice and Nathan Tinker, pp. 121–35. NY: Cambridge University Press, 2002.

——."Domestic Papers: Manuscript Culture and Early Modern Women's Life Writing." In *Genre and Women's Life Writing*, edited by Michelle M. Dowd and Julie A. Eckerle, pp. 33–48. Aldershot: Ashgate, 2007.

Feeley-Harnik, Gillian. "Cloth and the Creation of Ancestors in Madgascar." In *Cloth and Human Experience*, edited by Jane Schneider and Annette B. Weiner, pp. 73–116. Washington and London: Smithsonian Institution Press, 1989.

Feroli, Teresa. "'Infelix Simulacrum': The Rewriting of Loss in Elizabeth Jocelin's *The Mothers Legacie*." *ELH* 61 (1994): 89–102.

Field, Catherine. "'Many Many Hands:' Writing the Self in Early Modern Women's Recipe Books." In *Genre and Women's Life Writing*, edited by Dowd and Eckerle, pp. 49–63. Aldershot: Ashgate, 2007.

Fildes, Valerie, ed. *Women as Mothers in Pre-Industrial England*. New York: Routledge, 1990.

Flax, Jane. "Mother-Daughter Relationships: Psychodynamics, Politics, and Philosophy." In *The Future of Difference*, edited by Hester Eisenstein and Alice Jardine. Boston: G.K. Hall, 1980.

Fleming, Juliet. Review of *Writing Women in Jacobean England*, by Barbara Kiefer Lewalski. *The Huntington Library Quarterly* 57, no. 2 (1994): 199–204.

Folger MS X.d.428. The Cavendish-Talbot papers. The Folger Shakespeare Library. Washington, DC.

Fraser, Antonia. *Mary, Queen of Scots*. London: Weidenfield and Nicolson, 1987.

Friedman, Alice T. *House and Household in Elizabethan England: Wollaton House and the Willoughby Family*. Chicago: University of Chicago Press, 1989.

——. "Architecture, Authority, and the Female Gaze: Planning and Representation in the Early Modern Country House." *Assemblage* 18 (1992): 41–61.

——."Hardwick Hall." *History Today* 45, no. 1 (1995): 27–33.

Froide, Amy. "Marital Status as a Category of Difference." In *Singlewomen in the European Past*, edited by Judith M. Bennett and Amy M. Froide, pp. 236–69. Philadelphia: University of Pennsylvania Press, 1999.

Frye, Susan. *Elizabeth I: The Competition for Representation*. New York: Oxford University Press, 1993.

——."Sewing Connections: Elizabeth Tudor, Mary Stuart, Elizabeth Talbot, and Seventeenth Century Anonymous Needle Workers." In *Maids and Mistresses*, edited by Susan Frye and Karen Roberson, pp. 165–82. New York: Oxford University Press, 1999.

———. "Maternal Textualities." In *Maternal Measures: Figuring Caregiving in the Early Modern Period*, edited by Naomi J. Miller and Naomi Yavneh, pp. 224–36. Aldershot: Ashgate, 2000.

Frye, Susan and Karen Robertson, eds. *Maids and Mistresses, Cousins and Queens: Women's Alliances in Early Modern England*. New York: Oxford University Press, 1999.

Fumerton, Patricia, and Simon Hunt, eds. *Renaissance Culture and the Everyday*. Philadelphia: University of Pennsylvania Press, 1999.

Gilbert, Sandra. "Life's Empty Pack: Notes toward a Literary Daughteronomy." *Critical Inquiry* 11, no. 2 (1985): 255–84.

Gallagher, Catherine. "Embracing the Absolute: The Politics of the Female Subject in Seventeenth-Century England." *Genders* 1, no. 1 (1988): 24–39.

Greenblatt, Stephen. "Remnants of the Sacred in Early Modern England." In *Subject and Object in Renaissance Culture*, edited by Margreta de Grazia, Maureen Quilligan, and Peter Stallybrass, pp. 337–45. NY: Cambridge University Press, 1996.

Gristwood, Sarah. *Arbella: England's Lost Queen*. London: Bantam, 2004.

Guy, John. *Queen of Scots: The True Life of Mary Stuart*. Boston: Houghton Mifflin, 2004.

Hall, Kate. *A Material Girl: Bess of Hardwick, 1527–1608*. London: Short Books, 2001.

Hammons, Pamela. "The Gendered Imagination of Property in Sixteenth and Seventeenth-Century English Women's Verse." *Clio* 34, no. 4 (2005): 395–419.

———. "Rethinking Women and Property in Sixteenth- and Seventeenth-Century England." *Literature Compass* 3, no.6 (2006): 1386–1407.

Hanson, Elizabeth. "Boredom and Whoredom: Reading Renaissance Women's Sonnet Sequences." *Yale Journal of Criticism* 10, no. 1 (1997): 165–91.

Harris, Barbara J. "Property, Power, and Personal Relations: Elizabethan Mothers and Sons in Yorkist and Early Tudor England." *Signs* 51, no.3 (1990): 606–32.

———. *English Aristocratic Women 1450–1550: Marriage and Family, Property and Careers*. NY: Oxford University Press, 2002.

Harris, Olivia. "Households and their Boundaries." *History Workshop Journal* 13, (1982): 143–52.

Haugaard, William P. "The Coronation of Elizabeth I." *Journal of Ecclesiastical History* 19, no. 2 (1968): 161–70.

Heale, Elizabeth. "'Desiring Women Writing': Female Voices and Courtly 'Balets' in Some Early Tudor Manuscript Albums." In *Early Modern Women's Manuscript Writing*, edited by Victoria Burke and Jonathan Gibson, pp. 9–31. Aldershot: Ashgate, 2004.

Hedges, Elaine. "The Needle or the Pen: The Literary Rediscovery of Women's Textile Work." *Tradition and the Talents of Women*, edited by Florence Howe, pp. 338–64. Champaign: University of Illinois Press, 1990.

Hellwarth, Jennifer Wynne. "'I wyl wright of women prevy seknes': Imagining Female Literary and Textual Communities in Medieval and Early Modern Midwifery Manuals." *Critical Survey* 14 (2002): 33–60.

Henderson, Diana E. "Female Power and the Devaluation of Renaissance Love Lyrics." In *Dwelling in Possibility: Women Poets and Critics on Poetry*, edited by Yopie Prins and Maerra Shreiber, pp. 38–59. Ithaca: Cornell University Press, 1997.

Herman, Peter C. "Authority and the Royal 'I': King James VI/I and the Politics of Monarchic Verse." *Renaissance Quarterly* 54 (2001): 1495–1530.

———. "'Mes subjectz, mon ame assubjectie': The Problematic (of) Subjectivity in Mary Stuart's Sonnets." *Reading Monarchs Writing*, edited by Peter C. Herman, pp. 160–93. Tempe, AZ: MRTS, 2002.

Herman, Peter C., ed. *Reading Monarchs Writing: The Poetry of Henry VIII, Mary Stuart, Elizabeth I, and James VI/I*. Tempe, AZ: MRTS, 2002.

Hirsch, Marilyn. "Mothers and Daughters." *Signs* 7, no.1 (1981): 200–222.

Holm, Janis Butler. "The Myth of a Feminist Humanism: Thomas Salter's *The Mirrhor of Modestie*." In *Ambiguous Realities: Women in the Middle Ages and Renaissance*, edited by Carole Levin and Jeanie Watson, pp. 197–218. Detroit: Wayne State University Press, 1987.

Holmes, P.J. "Mary Stewart in England." In *Mary Stewart*, edited by Michael Lynch, pp. 195–218. Oxford: Blackwell, 1988.

Hosington, Brenda. "England's First Female-authored Encomium: The Seymour Sister's *Hecatodistichon* (1550) to Marguerite de Navarre. Text, Translation, Notes and Commentary." *Studies in Philology* 93 (1996): 117–63.

Hosington, Brenda, ed. *The Early Modern Englishwoman: A Facsimile Library of Essential Works*. Series 1. Printed Writings, 1500–1640. Part 2. vol. 6. Anne, Margaret, and Jane Seymour. Aldershot: Ashgate, 2000.

Howard, Alathea, Countess of Arundell. Letter to her grandmother Elizabeth Talbot. The Phillipps Collection (from MS 20556) Misc English. The Pierpont Morgan Library. New York, NY.

Idem Iterum, or, The History of Q. Mary's Big-Belly from Mr. Fox's Acts and Monuments and Dr. Heylin's Hist. Res. London, 1688.

James, Susan E. *Kateryn Parr: The Making of a Queen*. Aldershot: Ashgate, 1999.

Johnson, Barbara. "My Monster/My Self." *Diacritics* 12 (1982): 2–10.

Jones, Ann Rosalind. "Surprising Fame: Renaissance Gender Ideologies and Women's Lyric." In *The Poetics of Gender*, edited by Nancy K. Miller, pp. 74–95. NY: Columbia University Press, 1986.

———. *The Currency of Eros: Women's Love Lyric in Europe 1540–1620*. Bloomington: Indiana University Press, 1990.

———. "Maidservants of London: Sisterhoods of Kinship and Labor." In *Maids and Mistresses*, edited by Susan Frye and Karen Roberson, pp. 21–32. New York: Oxford University Press, 1999.

Jones, Ann Rosalind and Peter Stallybrass. *Renaissance Clothing and the Materials of Memory*. NY: Cambridge University Press, 2000.

Jourdain, Margaret. *The History of English Secular Embroidery*. London: Kegan Paul, 1910.

Kahn, Coppelia. "'Magic of Bounty': *Timon of Athens*, Jacobean Patronage, and Maternal Power." *Shakespeare Quarterly* 38, no. 1 (1987): 34–57.

Kendrick, A.F. *English Embroidery*. London: George Newnes Ltd., 1905.

King, John. "Patronage and Piety: The Influence of Catherine Parr." In *Silent but for the Word: Tudor Women as Patrons, Translators, and Writers of Religious Works*, edited by Margaret P. Hannay, pp. 43–60. Kent: Kent State University Press, 1985.

Klein, Lisa. "Lady Anne Clifford as Mother and Matriarch: Domestic and Dynastic Issues in Her Life and Writings." *Journal of Family History* 26, no. 1 (2001): 18–38.

——. "'Your Humble Handmaid': Elizabethan Gifts and Needlework." *Renaissance Quarterly* 50, no. 2 (1997): 459–94.

Knowles, James. "'Infinite Riches in a Little Room': Marlowe and the Aesthetics of the Closet." In *Renaissance Configurations: Voices/Bodies/Spaces, 1580–1690*, edited by Gordon McMullan, pp. 3–29. NY: St. Martin's Press, 1998.

Korda, Natasha. *Shakespeare's Domestic Economies: Gender and Property in Early Modern England*. Philadelphia: University of Pennsylvania Press, 2002.

——. "Singlewomen and the Properties of Poverty in *Measure for Measure*." In *Women, Property, and the Letters of the Law*, edited by Nancy E. Wright, et al., pp. 136–61. Toronto: University of Toronto Press, 2004.

Kuehn, Thomas J. "Understanding Gender Inequality in Renaissance Florence: Personhood and Gifts of Maternal Inheritance by Women." *Journal of Women's History* 8, no.2 (1996): 58–80.

Lanser, Susan. "Singular Politics: The Rise of the English Nation and the Production of the Old Maid." In *Singlewomen in the European Past*, edited by Judith M. Bennett and Amy Froide, pp. 297–323. Philadelphia: University of Pennsylvania Press, 1999.

Lanyer, Aemilia. "The Description of Cooke-ham." Rpt. in *Renaissance Women Poets*, edited by Danielle Clark. NY: Penguin, 2000.

Laslett, Peter. *The Household and Family in Past Time*. Cambridge: Cambridge University Press, 1972.

Levey, Santina M. *Elizabethan Treasures: The Hardwick Hall Textiles*. NY: Harry Abrams, 1998.

——. "References to Dress in the Earliest Account Book of Bess of Hardwick." *Costume: The Journal of the Costume Society* 34 (2000): 13–27.

——. *'Of Houshold stuff': the 1601 Inventories of Bess of Hardwick*. London: The National Trust, 2001.

Levin, Carole. "Sister-Subject/Sister-Queen: Elizabeth I among Her Siblings." In *Siblings and Gender in the Early Modern World: Sisters, Brothers, and Others*, edited by Naomi J. Miller and Naomi Yavneh, pp. 77–88. Aldershot: Ashgate, 2006.

Lewalski, Barbara Kiefer. *Writing Women in Jacobean England*. Cambridge: Harvard University Press, 1993.

Lipking, Lawrence. *The Life of the Poet: Beginning and Ending Poetic Careers*. Chicago: University of Chicago Press, 1981.

———. *Abandoned Women and Poetic Tradition*. Chicago: University of Chicago Press, 1988.

Loades. David. *Mary Tudor: A Life*. Oxford: Basil Blackwell, 1989.

Lovell, Mary. *Bess of Hardwick: Empire Builder*. NY: Norton, 2006.

Luecke, Marilyn. "The Reproduction of Culture and Culture of Reproduction in Elizabeth Clinton's *The Countesse of Lincolnes Nurserie*." In *Women, Writing, and the Reproduction of Culture*, edited by Mary E. Burke, et al., pp. 238–52. Syracuse: Syracuse University Press, 2000.

Lynch, Michael, ed. *Mary Stewart: Queen in Three Kingdoms*. Oxford: Blackwell, 1988.

Magnusson, Lyyne. *Shakespeare and Social Dialogue: Dramatic Language and Elizabethan Letters*. NY: Cambridge University Press, 1999.

———. "A Rhetoric of Requests: Genre and Linguistic Scripts in Elizabeth Women's Suitors' Letters." In *Women and Politics*, edited by James Daybell, pp. 51–66. Aldershot: Ashgate, 2004.

Mainardi, Patricia. "Quilts: The Great American Art." In *Feminism and Art History: Questioning the Litany*, edited by Norma Broude and Mary D. Garrard, pp. 331–46. Boulder, CO: Westview Press, 1982.

Marcus, Jane. "Still Practice/ A/Wrested Alphabet: Toward a Feminist Aesthetic." In *Feminist Issues in Literary Scholarship*, edited by Shari Benstock, pp. 79–97. Bloomington: Indiana University Press, 1987.

Marotti, Arthur. "'Love is not Love': Elizabethan Sonnet Sequences and the Social Order." *English Literary History* 49 (1982): 392–408.

Martin, Randall, ed. *Women Writers in Renaissance England*. NY: Longman, 1997.

Mary, Queen of Scots. *The Letters of Mary Stuart*. Edited by Prince Alexander Labanoff. Translated by William Turnbull. London: Charles Dolman, 1845.

———. *The Letters and Poems of Mary Stuart, Queen of Scots*. Translated by Clifford Bax. NY: Philosophical Library, 1947.

Matchinske, Megan. "Credible Consorts: What Happens When Shakespeare's Sisters Enter the Syllabus?" *Shakespeare Quarterly* (1996): 433–50.

Mauss, Marcel. *The Gift: The Form and Reason for Exchange in Archaic Societies*. NY: Norton, 2000.

Mazzola, Elizabeth. *The Pathology of the English Renaissance: Sacred Remains and Holy Ghosts*. Leiden and Boston: E.J. Brill, 1998.

———. "'O unityng confounding': Elizabeth I, Mary Stuart, and the Matrix of Renaissance Gender." *Exemplaria* 12 (2000): 385–416.

Merriman, M.H. "Mary, Queen of France." In *Mary Stewart*, edited by Michael Lynch, pp. 30–52.Oxford: Blackwell, 1988.

Michalove, Sharon D. "Equal in Opportunity? The Education of Aristocratic Women 1450–1550." In *Women's Education in Early Modern Europe: A History, 1500–1800*, edited by Barbara J. Whitehead, pp. 47–74. NY: Garland, 1999.

Miller, Naomi. "(M)other Tongues: Maternity and Subjectivity." In *Aemilia Lanyer: Gender, Genre, and the Canon*, edited by Marshall Grossman, pp. 143–66. Lexington: University Press of Kentucky, 1998.

Miller, Shannon. "Constructing the Female Self: Architectural Structures in Mary Wroth's *Urania*." In *Renaissance Culture and the Everyday*, edited by Patricia Fumerton and Simon Hunt, pp. 139–61. Philadelphia: University of Pennsylvania Press, 1999.

Mueller, Janel. "The Feminist Poetics of Aemilia Laner's *Salve Deus Rex Judaeorum*." In *Feminist Measures: Soundings in Poetry and Theory*, edited by Lynn Keller and Cristanne Miller, pp. 208–36. Ann Arbor: Michigan, 1994.

——."Virtue and Virtuality: Gender in the Self-Representations of Queen Elizabeth." In *Form and Reform in Renaissance England: Essays in Honor of Barbara Kiefer Lewalski*, edited by Amy Boesky and Mary Thomas Crane, pp. 220–46. Newark: University of Delaware Press, 2000.

Murphy, Erin. "Copulating with the Mother: *Paradise Lost* and the Politics of Begetting." (unpublished essay).

Nevanlimma, Saara. "The First Translation of a Young Princess: Holograph Manuscript versus Printed Text." In *Proceedings from the Third Nordic Conference for English Studies*. Vol. 1, edited by Ishrat Lindblad and Magnas Ljung. Stockholm, 1987.

Nevinson, John L. *Catalogue of English Domestic Embroidery of the Sixteenth and Seventeenth Centuries*. London: Victoria and Albert Museum Department of Textiles, 1938.

——. "New Year's Gifts to Queen Elizabeth 1584." *Costume: Journal of the Costume Society* 9 (1975): 27–31.

Newman, Karen. "City Talk: Women and Commodification in Jonson's *Epicoene*." *ELH* 56, no. 3 (1989): 503–18.

——. "Sundry Letters, Worldly Goods: The Lisle Letters and Renaissance Studies." *The Journal of Medieval and Early Modern Studies* 26, no. 1 (1996): 139–52.

Nochlin, Linda. "Why Have There Been No Great Women Artists?" In *Art and Sexual Politics*, edited by Thomas B. Hess and Elizabeth C. Baker, pp.1–39. NY: Macmillan, 1971.

Opie, Iona, and Peter Opie. *The Classic Fairy Tales*. Oxford: Oxford University Press, 1974.

Orlin, Lena Cowen. "The Fictional Families of Elizabeth I." In *Political Power, Rhetoric, and Renaissance Women*, edited by Carole Levin and Patricia A. Sullivan, pp. 85–110. Albany: SUNY Press, 1995.

——."Three Ways to be Invisible in the Renaissance: Sex, Reputation, and Stitchery." In *Renaissance Culture and the Everyday*, edited by Patricia Fumerton and Simon Hunt, pp. 183–203. Philadelphia: University of Pennsylvania Press, 1999.

Ostovich, Helen and Elizabeth Sauer, eds. *Reading Early Modern Women: An Anthology of Texts in Manuscript and Print*. NY: Routledge, 1994.

Parker, Roszika. *The Subversive Stitch: Embroidery and the Making of the Feminine.* NY: Routledge, 1984.

Parker, Rozsika, and Griselda Pollock. "Crafty Women and the Hierarchy of the Arts." In *Old Mistresses: Women, Art and Ideology*, pp. 50–81. NY: Pandora Press, 1991.

Paster, Gail Kerns. *The Body Embarrassed: Drama and the Disciplines of Shame in Early Modern England.* Ithaca: Cornell University Press, 1993.

Philippy, Patricia. "The Maid's Lawful Liberty: Service, the Household, and 'Mother B' in Isabella Whitney's 'A Sweet Nosgay.'" *Modern Philology* (1998): 439–62.

Phillips, James Emerson. *Images of a Queen: Mary Stuart in Sixteenth-Century Literature.* Berkeley: University of California Press, 1964.

Plowden, Alison. *The Elizabethan Secret Service.* NY: St. Martin's Press, 1991.

Pollock, Griselda. *Differencing the Canon: Feminist Desire and the Writing of Art's Histories.* London: Routledge, 1999.

Pollock, Linda "'Teach her to live under obedience': The Making of Women in the Upper Ranks of Early Modern England." *Continuity and Change* 4, no.2 (1989): 231–58.

Prescott, Anne Lake. "The Pearl of the Valois and Elizabeth I: Marguerite de Navarre's *Miroir* and Tudor England." In *Silent but for the Word: Tudor Women as Patrons, Translators, and Writers of Religious Works*, edited by Margaret P. Hannay, pp.61–76. Kent: Kent State UP, 1985.

Quilligan, Maureen. "Elizabeth's Embroidery." *Shakespeare Studies* 28 (2000): 218–25.

——. *Incest and Agency in Elizabeth's England.* Philadelphia: University of Pennsylvania Press, 2005.

——. "When Women Ruled the World: The Glorious Sixteenth Century." *Early Modern Culture: An Electronic Seminar* 5 (2006) http://emc.eserver.org/1–5.

Rich, Adrienne. *Of Woman Born: Motherhood as Experience and Institution* (1976). NY: Norton, 1986.

Richards, Judith M. "Mary Tudor as 'Sole Quene'? Gendering Tudor Monarchy." *Historical Journal* 40, no. 4 (1997): 895–924.

——. "Mary Tudor: Renaissance Queen of England." In *"High and Mighty Queens" of Early Modern England*, edited by Carole Levin, Debra Barrett-Graves, and Jo Eldridge Carney, pp. 27–42. NY: Palgrave Macmillan, 2003.

——. "The Two Tudor Queens Regnant." *History Review* (2005): 7–12.

Ring, Betty. "English Embroideries." In *Needlework: An Historical Survey*, edited by Betty Ring, pp. 10–13. NY: Main Street/Universe Books, 1975.

Rose, Mary Beth. "Where are the Mothers in Shakespeare? Options for Gender Representation in the English Renaissance." *Shakespeare Quarterly* 42, no.3 (1991): 291–314.

Ruddick, Sara. "Maternal Thinking." *Feminist Studies* 6, no.2 (1980): 342–67.

Salzman, Paul, ed. *Early Modern Women's Writing: An Anthology 1560–1700.* NY: Oxford University Press, 2000.

Scheman, Naomi. *Engenderings: Constructions of Knowledge, Authority, and Privilege*. NY: Routledge, 1993.

Schneider, Jane, and Annette B. Weiner, eds. *Cloth and Human Experience*. Washington and London: Smithsonian Institution Press, 1989.

Seymour, Anne, Margaret, and Jane. *The Hecatodistichon (1550–1551)*. Edited and translated by Patricia Demers (1999) in "The Seymour Sisters." *Sixteenth Century Journal* 30, no.2 (1999): 343–65.

Shell, Marc. *Elizabeth's Glass*. Lincoln: University of Nebraska Press, 1993.

Silvers, Anita. "Has Her(oine's) Time Now Come?" *Journal of Aesthetics and Art Criticism* 48, no. 4 (1990): 365–79.

Skura, Meredith. "The Reproduction of Mothering in *Mariam, Queen of Jewry*: A Defense of "Biographical' Criticism." *Tulsa Studies in Women's Literature* 16, no. 1 (1997): 27–56.

Snook, Edith. *Women, Reading, and the Cultural Politics of Early Modern England*. Aldershot: Ashgate, 2005.

Somerset, Anne. *Ladies-in-Waiting from the Tudors to the Present Day*. NY: Knopf, 1984.

——. *Elizabeth I*. NY: St. Martin's Press, 1991.

Starkey, David. *Elizabeth: The Struggle for the Throne*. NY: Harper Perennial, 2001.

Steen, Sara Jayne. "Fashioning an Acceptable Self: Arbella Stuart." *ELR* 18 (1988): 78–95.

——."Manuscript Matters: Reading the Letters of Lady Arbella Stuart." *South Central Review* 11, no. 2 (1994): 24–38.

——. "The Cavendish-Talbot Women: Playing a High Stakes Game." In *Women and Politics in Early Modern England*, edited by James Daybell, pp. 147–63. Aldershot: Ashgate, 2004.

Stevenson, Jane, and Peter Davidson, eds. *Early Modern Women Poets: An Anthology*. NY: Oxford University Press, 2001.

Stewart, Alan, and Heather Wolfe. *Letterwriting in Renaissance England*. Washington, DC, Seattle: The University of Washington Press, 2004.

Strathern, Marilyn. "Producing Gender Difference: Connections and Disconnections in Two New Guinea Highland Kinship Systems." In *Gender and Kinship: Essays Toward a Unified Analysis*, edited by J.F. Colier and S.J. Yanagisako, pp. 271–300. Stanford: Stanford University Press, 1987.

Stuart, Arbella. *The Letters of Lady Arbella Stuart*. Edited by Sara Jayne Steen. NY: Oxford University Press, 1994

Summit, Jennifer. "'The Arte of a Ladies Penne': Elizabeth I and the Poetics of Queenship." *ELR* 26 (1996): 395–422.

——. *Lost Property: The Woman Writer and English Literary History, 1380–1589*. Chicago: University of Chicago Press, 2000.

——."Writing Home: Hannah Wolley, the Oxinden Letters, and Household Epistolary Practice." In *Women, Property, and the Letters of the Law in Early Modern England*, edited by Nancy E. Wright, Margaret W. Ferguson, and A.R. Buck, pp. 201–18.Toronto: University of Toronto Press, 2004.

Swain, Margaret. *The Needlework of Mary, Queen of Scots*. New York: Van Nostrand Reinhold, 1973.

——. "A New Year's Gift from the Princess Elizabeth." *The Connoisseur* 183, no. 738 (1973): 258–66.

Synge, Lanto. *Art of Embroidery: History of Style and Technique*. Woodbridge, England: Antique Collectors' Club, 2001.

Teague, Frances. "Princess Elizabeth's Hand in *The Glass of the Sinful Soul*." In *Writings by Early Modern Women*, edited by Peter Beal and Margaret J.M. Ezell, pp.33–48. London: The British Library, 2000.

Travitsky, Betty S. "The New Mother of the English Renaissance: Her Writings on Motherhood." In *The Lost Tradition: Mothers and Daughters in Literature*, edited by Cathy N. Davidson and E.M. Bronner, pp. 33–43. New York: Ungar, 1980.

——."The 'Wyll and Testament' of Isabella Whitney." *ELR* 10, no. 1 (1980): 76–94.

——, ed. *The Paradise of Women: Writings by Englishwomen of the Renaissance*. NY: Columbia University Press, 1981.

——."The Possibilities of Prose." In *Women and Literature in Britain*, edited by Helen Wilcox, pp. 234–66. New York: Cambridge University Press, 1996.

——, ed. *Mother's Advice Books*. Volume 8. *The Early Modern Englishwoman: A Facsimile Library of Essential Works*. Printed Writings 1500–1640. Aldershot: Ashgate, 2001.

Travitsky, Betty S. and Anne Lake Prescott, eds. *Female and Male Voices in Early Modern England*. NY: Columbia University Press, 2000.

Ulrich, Laurel Thatcher. "Pens and Needles: Documents and Artifacts in Women's History." *Uncoverings: Research Papers of the American Quilt Society Study Group* 14 (1993): 221–28.

Vickers, Nancy J. "Diana Described: Scattered Woman and Scattered Rhyme." *Writing and Sexual Difference*, edited by Elizabeth Abel, pp. 95–109. Chicago: University of Chicago Press, 1982.

Vosevich, Kathi. "The Education of a Prince(ss): Tutoring the Tudors." In *Women, Writing, and the Reproduction of Culture*, edited by Mary Burke, et al., pp. 61–76. Syracuse: Syracuse University Press, 2000.

Wall, Wendy. "Isabella Whitney and the Female Legacy." *ELH* 58, (1991): 35–62.

——. *Staging Domesticity: Household Work and English Identity in Early Modern Drama*. NY: Cambridge University Press, 2002.

Warnicke, Retha. "Inventing the Wicked Women of Tudor England." *Quidditas* 20 (1999): 11–30.

Wayne, Valerie. "Advice for Women from Mothers and Patriarchs." In *Women and Literature in Britain*, edited by Helen Wilcox, pp. 56–79. New York: Cambridge University Press, 1996.

Weiner, Annette B. "Why Cloth? Wealth, Gender, and Power in Oceania." In *Cloth and Human Experience*, edited by Jane Schneider and Annette B. Weiner, pp. 33–72. Washington and London: Smithsonian Institution Press, 1989.

Wighigham, Frank. "The Rhetoric of Elizabethan Suitors' Letters." *PMLA* 96, no. 5 (1981): 864–82.

Bibliography

Whitehead, Barbara J., ed. *Women's Education in Early Modern Europe: A History, 1500–1800.* NY: Garland Publishing, 1999.

Whitney, Isabella. "WYLL and Testament." Rpt. in *Renaissance Women Poets.* Edited by Danielle Clark. NY: Penguin, 2000.

Wilcox, Helen, ed. *Women and Literature in Britain 1500-1700.* New York: Cambridge University Press, 1996.

——. "'Free and Easy as Ones Discourse?' Genre and Self-Expression in the Poems and Letters of Early Modern Englishwomen." In *Genre and Women's Life Writing*, edited by Michelle Dowd and Julie A. Eckerle, pp. 15–32. Aldershot: Ashgate, 2007.

Wilson, Carol Shiner. "Understanding Cultural Contexts: The Politics of Needlework in Taylor, Barbauld, Lamb, and Wordsworth." In *Approaches to Teaching British Women Poets of the Romantic Period*, edited by Stephen C. Behrendt and Harriet Kramer, pp. 80–84. NY: MLA Press, 1997.

Winkelmann, Carol L. "A Case Study of Women's Literacy in the Early Seventeenth Century: The Oxinden Family Letters." *Women and Language* 19, no. 2 (1996): 14–21.

Woodall, Joanna. "An Exemplary Consort: Antonis Mor's Portrait of Mary Tudor." *Art History* 14, no.2 (1991): 192–224.

Woolf, Virginia. *A Room of One's Own* (1929). New York: Harcourt Brace Jovanovich, 1981.

Wright, Nancy E., Margaret W. Ferguson, and A.R. Buck, eds. *Women, Property, and the Letters of the Law in Early Modern England.* Toronto: University of Toronto Press, 2004.

Yeandle, Laetitia. "A School for Girls in Windsor." *Medieval and Renaissance Drama in England* 17 (2005): 272–80.

Ziegler, Georgianna. "My Lady's Chamber: Female Space, Female Chastity in Shakespeare." *Textual Practice* 4, no.1 (1990): 73–100.

Index

Ajmar, Marta 18n
Arnold, Janet 34n, 35n, 36, 38, 40n, 95
Ashelford, Janet 43n
Ashley, Catherine (Kat) 30
Askew, Anne 24n

Batho, Gordon 54n
Bax, Clifford 55n, 66n, 68
Beilin, Elaine 19n, 43n
Bennett, Judith M. 5n, 92n
Bess of Hardwick 1, 3, 6, 18, 87, 90, 94–7, 98
    as estate manager 56, 73–4, 94, 99, 103–6
    expenses for her children 8
    household inventories of 5, 11, 76, 96, 102, 103–4
    letters to 98–9
    needlework of 11, 50, 55, 57, 59, 100–103
    as royal jailer 10, 72–6, 79–80, 93, 99–100
Bishop, Elizabeth 87, 105
Boleyn, Anne 22, 28
Bowden, Caroline 13n
Breight, Curt 83n
Brown, Elizabeth 54n
Brown, Georgia E. 23n, 24
Brown, Sylvia 10n, 41
Burke, Mary 55n, 66n

Callaghan, Dympna 18, 97
Carter, Alison 36n, 38n
Cary, Elizabeth 21, 86
Cavallo, Sandra 2n
Cavanagh, Sheila 19n
Cavendish, Margaret (Duchess of Newcastle) 52, 86
Cavendish, William (husband of Bess of Hardwick) 6, 100
Chan, Mary 98n
Chodorow, Nancy 8n, 18, 106

Clark, Danielle 104
Clarke, Elizabeth 89–90
Clifford, Lady Anne 3, 18–19, 89–90, 96
Clinton, Elizabeth (Countess of Lincoln) 9, 44–7, 84
cloth, and royal clothing 38, 43,
    "trauncelating" of 38–40, 95, 97
    and women's ties 9, 38, 42, 44, 94
Cole, Mary Hill 63n
Crawford, Julie 2n, 3, 29n, 78n,79n
Crawford, Patricia 46n

Darnley, Charles 4, 6, 100
Daybell, James 6, 75n, 98n,106n
de Grazia, Margreta 43
Demers, Patricia 20, 21n, 29
de Zulueta, Francis 53, 57n, 59n
Digby, George 53, 57n
Dolan, Frances 72n
Donaldson, Gordon 66n
Donawerth, Jane 4n, 45n, 46n, 92, 95, 106n
Dowd, Michelle M. 106
Duffy, Eamon 40n
Durant, David 6n, 76, 87n, 95n
Durkan, John 53n

Eckerlie, Julie 106
education, female 9, 13–14
Elizabeth I, 1, 3, 4, 30, 63, 69–70, 74–5,
    10, 13–17,
    friendship with Bess of Hardwick 6–7
    needlework of 10,19, 24, 53
    New Year's gifts to 95, 98
    relationship with Mary Tudor 9, 33–4, 39, 47
    ties to Katherine Parr 9, 13, 16, 19, 24–7, 28, 34, 63, 82, 84
    writings of 14, 21, 9, 13, 16, 19–20, 22–7, 30–31, 33–4, 54, 82
    For imprisonment of Mary, Queen of Scots, *see* Stuart, Mary
Ellinghausen, Laurie 89n, 104n

124 Women's Wealth and Women's Writing in Early Modern England

Ellis, Margaret 56n, 57n,100n,102n, 106
Erasmus 44
Erickson, Amy 2n, 38, 92n
Erickson, Carrolly 35
Ezell, Margaret J. M. 8n, 72n,73n, 83n, 84, 90, 92–3

Fane, Rachel 13, 14, 21
Feeley-Harnik, Gillian 42, 43, 46
Feroli, Teresa 38n, 43n, 44
Field, Catherine 79n
Finch, Anne 52
Fleming, Juliet 8n, 55, 70, 90n
Fraser, Antonia 66n
Friedman, Alice T. 74n, 87n, 103n
Froide, Amy 5n, 16, 92
Frye, Susan 2n, 15, 16, 36n, 40, 47, 53n, 57, 63, 87n, 102n
Fumerton, Patricia 56n

Gallagher, Catherine 84.
gift-exchange 4, 53, 95, 98. *See also* women's wealth, circulation of
Gilbert, Sandra 31
Gouge, William 44
Greenblatt, Stephen 40n
Grey, Lady Catherine 1, 85
Grey, Lady Jane 1, 81, 85
Gristwood, Sarah 5, 10n, 74n,75n,86, 91n
Grymeston, Elizabeth 41, 44, 45
Guy, John 69, 71–3

Hall, Kate 87n
Hammons, Pamela 73n, 90n, 93, 107n
Hanson, Elizabeth 66n, 67n, 68n, 69
Harris, Barbara. 3n, 4n, 7–8, 71n, 72n, 73n, 77n, 92, 99
Haugaard, William P. 40
Heale, Elizabeth 16n
Hedges, Elaine 50n
Hellwarth, Jennifer 2n
Henderson, Diana E. 67, 68n
Herman, Peter 54n, 55n, 68–9
Hirsch, Marilyn 95n
Holm, Janis Butler 14
Holmes, P.J. 50n
Hosington, Brenda 20

household
    early modern rules governing 4, 56, 71–3
    as linked with private space 49, 54
    as rival court 103
    as site of discipline 72–4, 76
    and women's responsibilities 40–41, 45, 52, 71–2
Howard, Alathea (Talbot) 17–18

Idem Iterum, or, the history of Q. Mary's big belly 34–5
Irigaray, Luce 46

James, Susan 13n, 19n, 29n
Jefferies, Joyce 105
Jocelin, Elizabeth 10, 41, 43
Johnson, Barbara 38n
Jones, Ann Rosalind 49, 61, 65, 92
    and Peter Stallybrass 9, 34, 39, 40, 42, 44
Jonson, Ben 57, 88
Jourdain, Margaret 53, 59n

Kahn, Coppelia 82n
Kendrick, A.F. 56n
King, John 4n, 28n
Klein, Lisa 3, 8n, 24n, 50n, 53n, 93n, 95
Knowles, James 54n
Korda, Natasha 2n, 38, 40–41, 72n, 94n
Kuehn, Thomas J. 2n, 3, 78, 93–4

Lanser, Susan 92n
Lanyer, Aemilia 4, 11, 87–90, 92, 96–7, 107
Leigh, Dorothy 9, 41
Lennox, Margaret 6
Levey, Santina 5n, 6n, 74n, 76n, 100n, 102n, 103
Levin, Carole 34
Lewalski, Barbara 73n, 74n, 75n, 90n
Lipking, Lawrence 57, 67, 106
literacy, early modern definitions of 2
    and women 91
Loades, David 34n, 36
Lodge, Thomas 44
Lovell, Mary 6, 49, 76, 87n, 103
Luecke, Marilyn 45–6
Lynch, Michael 55n, 66n

Index

property. *See* wealth, women's

Magnusson, Lynne 78
Mainardi, Patricia 8n, 50n
Marcus, Jane 65, 67
Marotti, Arthhur 66–8
Martin, Randall 45n
Mary of Guise 5
Mary Tudor 5–6, 30, 33–4, 39, 41, legacy
    to Elizabeth 33, 35, 36, 39, 47
Matchinske, Megan 93n
Merriman, M.H 63
Michalove, Sharon 14n
Miller, Naomi 90n, 96, 97n
Miller, Shannon 74n
Milton, John 22
motherhood
    early modern ideas surrounding 7, 11,
        33, 35
    early modern "rewritings" of 9, 16, 19,
        21–2, 27–31, 34, 41, 45, 47, 96, 97
    modern "domestications" of 7–8
mothers' advice books 21, 27, 33, 41, 43.
    See also women's writing.
Mueller, Janel 54, 61
Mulcaster, Richard 14
Murphy, Erin 22

Navarre, Marguerite de 5, 16, 19, 20–31
needlework 46–7, 51–3, 55
    and education 14–15
    feminization of 55–6, 57, 63
Nevanlimma, Saara 19n
Nevinson, John L. 61n, 95n
Newman, Karen 2n, 3

Opie, Iona and Peter Opie 36n
Orlin, Lena Cowen 49n, 50n, 55–6, 63
Ostovich, Helen 106n

Parker, Roszika 50n, and Griselda Pollock
    2n, 56
Parr, Katherine 5, 13, 19–20, 27–9
Paster, Gail Kerns 46n, 47n
Philippy, Patricia 79n
Phillipps, James Emerson 70n
Plowden, Alison 6n
Pollock, Linda 71n
Prescott, Anne Lake 19n, 21n, 26, 29n, 30n

Quilligan, Maureen 16n, 19n, 21n, 24, 30,
    31n, 42n, 44n, 51, 96, 102n

Rich, Adrienne 7, 30, 94n
Richards, Judith 39
Ring, Betty 14n
Ruddick, Sara 95n

Salter, Thomas 13–14
Sauer, Elizabeth 106n
Scheman, Naomi 28
Schneider, Jane 42–3
Seymour, Anne, Jane, and Margaret 9, 20,
    22, 27, 29–31
Seymour, Edward (Earl of Hertford, son
    of the Lord Protector) 1, 7, 75, 78,
    81–4
Seymour, Edward (Lord Protector) 20,
    28–30
Seymour, Jane (Jane Seimer) 85
Seymour, Thomas (Lord Admiral) 19–20,
    28, 29n, 30, 84
Seymour, William 7, 85, 94
Shakespeare
    William and *Antony and Cleopatra*
        21, 47
    Coriolanus 49, 51
    Hamlet 38, 49n
    King Lear 11, 42–3, 68, 97
    Macbeth 35, 38
    Othello 2n, 41, 97, 106
    The Taming of the Shrew 41
    The Winter's Tale 2n, 11, 21, 41, 80
Shell, Marc 26
Silvers, Anita 61n
singlewomen. *See* women's status as
    singlewomen.
Skura, Meredith 21n
Smythson, Robert 87
Snook, Edith 4n, 14n, 24n, 84
Somerset, Anne 34n, 95n
St. Loe, Sir William 6
Stallybrass, Peter. *See* Jones, Ann Rosalind.
Stanhope, Anne 20, 28
Starkey, David 34n, 54n

Index

Steen, Sara Jayne 1n, 10n, 71, 75n, 85–6, 91n, 98n
Steward, Alan 78
Strathern, Marilyn 3n, 78, 85
Stuart, Lady Arbella 1, 4, 6–7, 10–11, 40, 75–6, 91–6, 103–7
   letters of 10, 72–86, 91, 99, 103, 106
Stuart, Mary (Mary, Queen of Scots) 4, 6–7, 40, 49, 53, 69–72, 74, 99–100
   needlework of 6, 10, 11, 50–66, 69, 86, 100
   writings of 50–52, 65, 66–70
Summit, Jennifer 2, 8, 24, 50n, 54n, 70n, 81
Swain, Margaret 10n, 24, 40, 52, 53n, 56n, 57n, 59, 100
Synge, Lanto 24n

Talbot, Elizabeth (Countess of Shrewsbury). *See* Bess of Hardwick.
Talbot, George (Earl of Shrewsbury) 4, 6, 98, 100
Talbot, Mary 91, 94, 100
Teague, Frances 27
Thomas, Yan 93
Travitsky, Betty 35, 43n, 44, 45n, 66n, 89n, 104n

Ulrich, Laurel Thatcher 50n

Vickers, Nancy 51
Vosevich, Kathi 19n

Wall, Wendy 2n, 7, 43, 72, 76, 78, 89n, 104n
Warnicke, Retha 28
Wayne, Valerie 27, 73
Weiner, Annette 42–3, 44n, 46, 96n
Whigham, Frank 79
Whitehead, Barbara J. 71n

Whitney, Isabella 11, 31, 40, 46–7, 79n, 87–91, 94–5, 104–5, 106n
Wilcox, Helen 75n
Wilson, Carol Shiner 56n
Wingfield, Elizabeth 98
Winkellmann, Carol L. 91
Wolfe, Heather 78
women's networks 8
   influence of 93–9
   as a world of readers and writers 4, 92–3
women's status as singlewomen 5, 11, 79, 92, 94, 96, 104–6
women's wealth
   circulation of 33, 35, 38, 41–4, 95–6, 107
   and the manipulation of kin ties 5, 38, 85, 92–3
women's writings
   as "housework" 77–9
   as index of kin ties 8–9, 10, 16, 18, 21, 78, 79, 84–5, 96
   as managing wealth 2–3, 8, 11, 77, 88, 90, 92
   as material objects 1–2, 73, 78, 83
   and the "problem" of the woman writer 11, 70, 77, 83–4
   and questions of "authorship" 55, 81
   as response to Petrarchism 66–7
Woodall, Joanna 33, 38n
Woolf, Virginia 2n, 11, 36, 41–2, 83, 94, 107
Wright, Nancy E. 98n
Wroth, Lady Mary 67, 86, 96

Yeandle, Laetitia 13

Ziegler, Georgianna 49

CPSIA information can be obtained
at www.ICGtesting.com
Printed in the USA
BVHW040032250119
538623BV00009B/128/P